AWAKE

YOUR INTUITIVE VISION

Unlocking possibilities you never knew existed

Mary Nondé

Dear Kenda

Thank you for your contribution
— always delightful — to this
work and this book.
Love Mary 18/01/19

Printed in the United Kingdom
First Printing, 2018

ISBN: 978-1-9164894-4-8 (Print edition)
ISBN: 978-1-9164894-5-5 (eBook Edition)

Librotas Books
Portsmouth, Hampshire
UK
PO2 9NT

www.Librotas.com

Contents

Acknowledgements

My first round of thanks goes to book mentor Karen Williams, for helping me create the framework that eventually became this book. Without your consistent and constructive support over the two and a half year interlude, I wouldn't have discovered what this book was *really* about. My gratitude to good friend Kate Pichon, for suggesting I contact Karen *even before* I had considered writing a book – and to my intuition for acting on this prompt with a resounding YES! And to the editor, Louise Lubke Cuss, designer Samantha Pearce, illustrator Jannah Nichol Kalkwarf, and photographer Tara Taylor for making it sound and look wonderful.

My dear friends Margaret Roselaar and Catherine Blackfeather, without your considerable generosity I would not have survived the most difficult and protracted period of my life or be in a place to write at all. Your kindness is such a blessing. And to my friends Doreen Gowing and Emily Wright, for believing in me and encouraging me when I was moaning and groaning. Also to my coach, Lindsey Wheeler, for listening well, cutting to the chase and holding my focus.

To all my teachers, the organic movement and somatic arts pioneers, who have dedicated their lives to this relatively new field of embodied practice: Miranda Tuffnell, Northumbria UK; Helen Poynor, Devon UK; Claude Coldy, Italy; Anna Halprin, California USA; and my tutor, Dr Jill Hayes, University of Chichester, whose innovative MA pathway in Somatic Arts Psychotherapy provided the intellectual framework for this book.

To my many clients, a massive thank you for your willingness to make Intuitive Vision Boards with me and participate in the coaching sessions that followed. Without you I would not have been able to appreciate the full value of this creative visioning process or how it can transform lives.

Finally, to my beautiful daughter Celine, who has accompanied me along the road less travelled and provided me with the motivation for taking it. I am very grateful for your presence and your considerable editing skills – of both my words and my clothes! And to my ever-faithful Labrador, Willow, always ready to accompany me whenever I needed the inspiration of nature to get me moving again – a big hug and a woof.

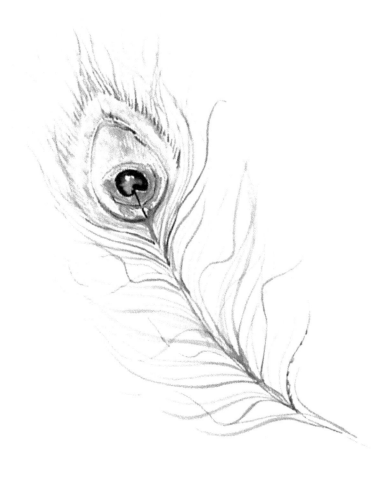

INTRODUCTION

01: Initiation

02: Invocation

03: Invention

04: Inception

05: Immersion

06: Illumination

07: Integration

08: Inauguration

From dark to sparkling light

"Harsh" is the best way to describe this chapter in my life that began in 2012. Over a six-month period I faced a whole catalogue of difficulties, one after the other. I watched incredulously as the cornerstones of my existence were callously uprooted, yet each loss was beyond my control. Like a battlefield after the soldiers have gone, I was left flattened.

In a state of shock and fear, with no money in my purse or in the bank, I waited for the next tax credit to arrive. I survived on supermarket basics and discovered discount stores to be a godsend. The word "loser" kept ringing in my ears. At the same time, it was a humbling experience to discover I was not alone in having to live this way.

I share this tale of woe not to labour it, nor as a victim, but as a reminder to all of us that misfortune comes in many shapes and sizes, and no-one is impervious.

I am a white, well-educated, middle-class woman. At the time I was 56 years old with my daughter still at school when I lost everything except, thankfully, her. No spring chicken with my future endlessly stretching ahead of me, I faced the prospect of rebuilding my existence from scratch. My family were quick to retract and unwilling to help, so I was alone with the financial and practical repercussions of our predicament. I felt crushed by the enormity of the task but the responsibilities were mine and that I accepted.

Resurrection from the ashes is possible and every cloud has a silver lining; I am evidence of both clichés being true. Besides, it's times like these, when life reduces you to a pulp, that can also initiate unprecedented personal transformation. So take heart if you are deep in the belly of adversity or know someone dear to you who is. Or maybe you're plain stuck at a crossroads, not able to decide which direction to go next. Either way, help is at hand.

In this book, I share what I've learnt about predicament from the benefit of hindsight and demonstrate that even in the darkest of circumstances there is light. I will tell you about the genius that turned my life around – the Intuitive Vision Board – and how it can do the same for you, whatever your circumstances, when you draw upon this life-affirming, inspirational tool.

The Intuitive Vision Board can be your lifeline and game-changer. It draws on resources you already have in your possession to *awaken* your intuition and *unlock* possibilities you never knew existed by turning a large, apparently serendipitous collection of images into an evocative collage to transform your life. What a surprise to discover that your intuition, imagination and creativity in combination can produce such an outcome. And an even greater surprise to discover the very same latent intuitive ability will also steer you a pathway through the maze and help you to manifest what you really need next but are unable to see or anticipate in advance.

In the first chapter I'll continue to elaborate on my personal journey. Throughout this book are interspersed real-life stories from people who have already benefitted from this amazing creative process. Their experiences of awakening intuitive vision and the consequences of doing so make fascinating reading, although their names and identities have been altered to preserve confidentiality.

I will take you through the process of making an Intuitive Vision Board. I will also share the psychology and philosophy behind it. I recommend you read the book from start to finish, in chronological order; then the step-by-step guide to making the board itself will make the most sense to you in Chapter 5.

I know you'll enjoy reading *Awaken Your Intuitive Vision* and will find yourself turning to your vision board for inspiration and returning to this book to create future vision boards, even at less complex moments in your life.

01: Initiation
02: Invocation
03: Invention
04: Inception
05: Immersion
06: Illumination
07: Integration
08: Inauguration

01: Initiation

02: Invocation

03: Invention

04: Inception

05: Immersion

06: Illumination

07: Integration

08: Inauguration

"That which does not kill us makes us stronger."

Friedrich Nietzsche, Philosopher

02: Invocation

03: Invention

04: Inception

05: Immersion

06: Illumination

07: Integration

08: Inauguration

Chapter 1

INITIATION

02: Invocation

03: Invention

04: Inception

05: Immersion

06: Illumination

07: Integration

08: Inauguration

Adversity defeats logic

The trouble is when you're facing adversity or there are difficult decisions to be made, the usual thought processing you rely upon can get muddled by emotion or, worse still, stop functioning altogether. When you are anxious, afraid or sad, you literally can't think straight and it's impossible to obtain the clarity you need. And if it's a complex problem with many parameters that won't rally together nicely to exit single file out of the corral, they can scatter your attention all over the place. Certainly this was my experience. And if your current attitude or behaviour has contributed to your arriving at this particular crossroads, it won't be that easy to disentangle your thinking to reach a new and different perspective, especially while you are still in it. Your thoughts will go around in circles while your head spins upon its axis.

One of two things can happen next without a third alternative. You can either react by flying into over-activity, throwing everything you've got at the situation in the hope that something good will come of it. Or you pull a paper bag over your head and do nothing at all, hoping the situation will miraculously disappear by the time you remove it. To mask how vulnerable you're *actually* feeling, you might also have recourse to the usual cocktail of avoidance tricks we're all familiar with: overeating, drinking, drugs (prescriptive and non-prescriptive), TV, internet, shopping... you name it. My particular form of coping, which I only realised later, was to remain in a co-dependent relationship years longer than I should have, hoping it would get better.

It is a precarious moment when your heart breaks and hangs by a thread. Or you're down on your luck and mightily confused. There is a risk this can crush your spirit too, which is why you must give yourself something spiritually uplifting to do. Paradoxically, it's in these moments of intense fragility that both the heart and mind can break free of limitation and convention and are at liberty to have new adventures; what is there to lose? This is not to minimise the challenges still to be dealt with or the decisions yet to be taken, but to encourage you to engage with creative alternatives, which have their foundations in a new reality, as yet sketchy and unclear (which is the nature of the beast).

Awakening your intuitive vision is the creative method I prescribe, which can offer you precisely that. A healthy alternative to procrastination in providing a creative outlet for the life force that still wants to flow through you, even when the outer structures of your life want to fall – or have already fallen – away. The difference between using the Intuitive Vision Board to enable this and many other personal development tools is that

13

01: Initiation

02: Invocation

03: Invention

04: Inception

05: Immersion

06: Illumination

07: Integration

08: Inauguration

you are not required to think up the answers. The answers are coming to you, as this book seeks to explain.

Sleeping giant

When I was in my darkest moments and at my most confused, I called upon a number of self-help practices to silence the incessant chatter inside my head and create headspace to navigate my way from despair to hope. I invite you to try any of these. They included free-flow writing and drawing every morning with my first cup of tea; walking outside in nature with the dog; and attending yoga classes regularly. However, the turnaround only occurred for me after I'd created my Intuitive Vision Board. I'd been working with vision boards regularly for several years prior to this but it was only when calamity struck that the potency of the process I'd created became evident – and I've been a passionate advocate ever since. Put it this way. If it could resolve a mess like the one I was in, then the Intuitive Vision Board could certainly help people find answers and a way through less complexity, as the stories woven throughout the book illustrate.

The secret ingredient to my approach lies not in the finished product, whereby all vision boards look much the same on the surface of things – a collage of pictures representing hopes and dreams. The catalyst lies in the way the vision is arrived at, by calling upon your intuition exclusively. With the Intuitive Vision Board the maker is tasked to park Logical-Left-brain thinking, because when you're emotionally ruffled you can't think straight anyway, to make way for a conversation with your right brain – and your intuition, imagination and creativity. I refer to these halves of the brain throughout as Remarkable-Right (RR-brain) and Logical-Left (LL-brain) to differentiate the two. Let me say right away this segmentation of the brain into two halves is perhaps more simplistic and metaphorical than actual but it provides a working model that's readily understood.

Everyone has one of each hemisphere, so there is no excuse to ignore Remarkable-Right, which lies dormant in most like a sleeping giant. Just because it's sleeping doesn't mean it can't be stirred with a playful prod. The questionable confusion that attends your standing at a crossroads is the perfect occasion to do so because residing in the underutilised capacity of Remarkable-Right lies the probability of an innovative pathway through the dilemma, which can also heal your heart and restore your love of life.

01: Initiation

14

02: Invocation

03: Invention

04: Inception

05: Immersion

06: Illumination

07: Integration

08: Inauguration

The Intuitive Vision Board provides a comfortable connection to your RR-brain without undue effort (for those of you who are already muttering you don't have one). This RR-brain field of intelligence, now awakened, is more expansive and evolutionary than the cognitive intelligence of LL-brain alone, which you use to organise and operate your daily life. If you have already forgotten your RR-brain exists, that is understandable. By the time you're an adult most statutory education will have drilled it out of you. Like most, you'll have been taught to think and learn in a linear fashion and to look for the one right answer that scores the mark. And heaven forbid if you can't show your workings and prove your findings, because your answer won't count.

Can you see how this approach is hopeless when you're conflicted? First, you have to be in a rational frame of mind to begin with, which you're not when you're under pressure. Second, there is no one correct answer to be found and if you pull a solution out of the bag too soon, the chances are it contains shortcomings and will need to be abandoned later.

The good news is, with little or no education in Remarkable-Right thought processing, you *still* have a right brain and can engage it in the creation of the Intuitive Vision Board. However, if you are well educated, there is every chance your RR-brain has already shrivelled to the size of a pea, metaphorically speaking. But there's nothing to worry about because I'll guide you through this creative process in such a way to resuscitate your Remarkable-Right while quietening your Logical-Left.

Decline and fall

So what exactly was it that brought me to my knees? And why was it so complex that my Logical-Left was unable to cope, while engaging my Remarkable-Right with the Intuitive Vision Board could help me to find resolution? This is the first step in the creative process called *Initiation*: recognising where you are stuck, how it's hurting and what is at stake if you remain there.

In my case I faced seven losses almost simultaneously. One at a time I could have managed, perhaps. But a fresh upset would appear before I had chance to resolve the last, each one compounding the previous, until I felt I was playing a leading role in a saga. If you are the kind of person who would not have been phased by any of them, where were you? I could have done with you at that time. If you recognise yourself, a friend, or family

02: Invocation

03: Invention

04: Inception

05: Immersion

06: Illumination

07: Integration

08: Inauguration

member in any one of these scenarios – and it helps in some way – then the tough lessons I learnt will have been worth sharing, which I do now with complete transparency.

Security ~ *Loss 1*

It all started with my partner ending our relationship. Fair enough, he wanted out. But then I discovered to my astonishment, even though we'd been co-habiting for ten years, that I had no entitlement.

It's a quirk of English law, which isn't the case I believe elsewhere, that because I had not contributed to a mortgage (there wasn't one) or added bricks and mortar to the house (he wouldn't let me create an extension), the contribution I had made counted for nothing. All the myriad ways I'd benefitted the home would only compute if I produced evidence: supermarket receipts, utility bills, cash receipts... Can you imagine what a soul-destroying task that would have been unless you were a natural hoarder? I am a Feng Shui professional so I'm not. Please learn from my mistake.

Home ~ *Loss 2*

So it came to pass that my ex retained all the capital and assets while my daughter and I left home empty-handed. There is an expression used to describe this outcome: 'unconscious uncoupling'.

Overnight we downsized from our four-bedroom detached home in leafy suburbia to a two-bed rented terrace on a noisy road. It was left entirely to me to purchase the second-hand furniture we needed for it and move house, while my ex sat tight in our old home. "This is so unfair!" I felt like screaming.

Income ~ *Loss 3*

We'd been running a business together, but I'd never taken an independent salary from it. Please be warned. This creates a massive roadblock when it comes to renting. To afford a modest two-bedroom home at that time, I needed to show a £35,000 salary or equivalent profit. Gasp! Or produce a guarantor (my wealthy father refused point blank). Or provide six months' rent in advance, on top of two months' deposit – about £10,000 in total. Another gasp! Because I'd sunk my entire savings into the family over the years and the rest in a loan to a friend, I didn't have this either. Eventually my ex found the deposit needed, otherwise he'd have been stuck with us forever.

01: Initiation   02: Invocation   03: Invention   04: Inception   05: Immersion   06: Illumination   07: Integration   08: Inauguration

16

Stability ~ *Loss 4*

It took me *19 attempts* to find a rental property which met all three of my criteria:

1. I could afford it.
2. It had public transport to school.
3. It would accept the dog. Yes, the dog. Pets and renting don't go well together, I discovered.

I took the first house that met all three criteria – but I didn't like it. During the next five years we moved *five more times*, mostly for financial reasons, and with all the effort and expense that takes. I certainly put my Feng Shui skills to the test.

Future prospects ~ *Loss 5*

At the time of moving out, a friend had told me about a property investment in the Caribbean, which offered a much greater return on investment than a normal pension fund. (I bet the hairs on the back of your neck are rising already.) Panicked as I was about my financial future, I transferred my modest, frozen pension fund into a SIP scheme called Harlequin. The name is ironic. The builder of these magnificent hotels turned out to be a complete clown. He bankrupted the company, and small-time investors like myself lost everything. Now with barely any cash in my purse or money in the bank, I had no security for the future either. If you think that's challenging enough, it gets worse.

Trust ~ *Loss 6*

Some years before the break-up, I'd received a legacy from my aunt worth £40,000. A very good friend had pleaded with me to loan them most of this to help to pay their bills while they were going through a difficult period – but on the promise it would be repaid. I trusted them. I believed them to be going through depression and I had compassion for their predicament. I later discovered this person to have a variety of personal and mental health problems. Would I have loaned my entire savings if I'd known? That's right, no.

Please note, dear readers, it also never occurred to me to get the loan in writing. Despite repeated efforts the money was never returned. I couldn't reclaim it through the Small Claims because *they* could afford a solicitor and I couldn't even afford to commence the procedure. I felt SO stupid.

17

01: Initiation

02: Invocation

03: Invention

04: Inception

05: Immersion

06: Illumination

07: Integration

08: Inauguration

Remaining parent ~ *Loss 7*

In the final curtain call in this challenging series my father died. When I last saw him alive, he stole a moment to tell me: "*My* family will be alright because we own more than 30 properties between us. But you will have failed your daughter because you have nothing to pass on to her." What did he mean?

Two months later he died. In his private game of Monopoly, his properties had been transferred to my step-family to avoid inheritance tax and to exclude my brother and I. Not a penny came our way. On top of the natural grief at losing my father, this rejection was a heart-breaking moment. And ironic too since without the security provided by my *mother's* parents to my father, he would not have been able to commence building his empire in the first place.

Why did my father choose to cut me out? I was hardly a wayward daughter and I can only speculate about his motivations. My father's value system was based almost exclusively around money and business. Because I had neither and was not married to somebody who did, I suspect he regarded me as a waste of space, which was his justification for disinheriting me.

However, on top of the six previous challenges, this one finally broke the camel's back and I crumbled with adrenal gland exhaustion – palpitations, night sweats, insomnia and fatigue – and these symptoms were to rattle me for another year.

Can you now see how complex the situation was? How could I devise a plan to negotiate a way through it all, especially when I was feeling so sad and dejected? And where was I to start?

Road to recovery

Once we'd settled into our new home, the reality of my diminishment set in. I'd wake up each morning in the tiny single bedroom, with the high window that looked out onto a towering brick wall, and wonder what I had done to arrive in this prison. I drifted through the early days on automatic and considered my greatest daily achievements to prepare a meal for us to eat together and walk the dog. My life was very simple. I didn't have the energy to take on a full-time job or do the work for which I had trained. I learned

01: Initiation

18

02: Invocation

03: Invention

04: Inception

05: Immersion

06: Illumination

07: Integration

08: Inauguration

quickly to survive on very little, but even so we were living from hand to mouth. Until one day a dear friend said: "Mary, here is my supermarket account number. Spend £50 a month and stock up your store cupboard." Her kindness took my breath away and, for the first time since the crisis began, I no longer felt alone.

Life is in a continuous state of flux and change is the consequence; that much we do know. If we're reluctant to accept this then we should consult with the quantum physicist. Our circumstances come and go. Making an Intuitive Vision Board is a fantastic way to stay attuned to these invisible undercurrents and locate your position in the grand scheme of things.

That's why three months into my new life and I was ready to make a new Intuitive Vision Board. Amazingly in the big picture I created, there was no trace of the hardship, heartbreak or hopelessness that I was experiencing at the time – and not because I deliberately avoided using such imagery. The creative process was naturally guiding me towards possibilities that would get me out of the hole and not keep me in it.

Here are some features of the new vision board I created:

Yoga teacher

Right in the centre of my Intuitive Vision Board was the oldest female *yoga teacher* in the world: Tao Porchon-Lynch. Here was a visual anchor I could return to again and again. It prompted me to take respite in yoga on the days when I felt I could do little else – despite Logical-Left yelling in my ear that I could afford neither the time nor the money for it. I loved the way Tao reached for the heavens while seated firmly on the earth. I was reassured by her age, still alive and practising her art at 94 years old, that there was time left ahead for me.

Floating

The woman *floating* on her back in the middle of a lake was a complete mystery. But I admired the way she appeared totally at peace with herself and at one with the elements. It was comforting to imagine how this might feel in my own body, to be this tranquil and supported.

02: Invocation

03: Invention

04: Inception

05: Immersion

06: Illumination

07: Integration

08: Inauguration

Ocean

There were three separate images of the *ocean* pasted next to the floating goddess, which I related to as my love of the sea. But why the vast ocean and not the sheltered coves I was accustomed to swimming in while growing up in Devon, I didn't know.

Seahorse

The *seahorse* right next to the ocean spoke to me of a handsome, singular creature: the male that is versatile and carries all the eggs in his pouch. Not many of those males in my life at the time.

Live, Love, Teach

The women creating around the kitchen table and the words *"Live, Love, Teach"* alongside encouraged me to return to my original intention to implement the training I had received from the MA in Somatic Arts Psychotherapy. But I had no branding, no website, no social media presence, and no money to afford any of these.

Flowers

The colourful *garden of flowers* surrounding the women provided encouragement that my life would bloom again as I helped other people's gardens to flourish, metaphorically speaking of course.

Daniel Craig

And there's *Daniel Craig* striding through the waves towards me. Only a question of time, I thought, before he'd come to my rescue...

01: Initiation

20

02: Invocation

03: Invention

04: Inception

05: Immersion

06: Illumination

07: Integration

08: Inauguration

Nine months passed...

Nine months later and I'm already in a better head-heart space. Little had changed on the surface of things but much repair work had taken place beneath. I'm drawn to attend a tango workshop where I'm paired with a complete stranger. Only the day before I'd had a fleeting thought that I would start looking for part-time work to supplement my income and fund my business. We chatted in the break. This man had his own company and I asked if he knew anyone who needed a part-time employee. He wasn't looking but offered me a trial, and I subsequently worked there for several years.

I didn't fully appreciate the significance of this encounter at the time except that I was grateful for the work. However, it transpired that I'd grasped the golden thread that would lead me to higher ground and yet I'd constellated this scenario on my vision board *nine months earlier*! This not only demonstrated to me the ability of Remarkable-Right to resolve complex problems long before Logical-Left could compute what the problems were and where to begin, but it also highlighted the precognitive capability of the Intuitive Vision Board.

Consider those key images again in a slightly different order...

Ocean... My new boss had an international floatation company called "*Ocean* Float Rooms".

Floating... My job was to sell the bliss and longevity of *floating* in a floatation room to individuals and well-being centres around the world.

Daniel Craig... My new boss had the muscular body and craggy looks (somewhat) of *Daniel Craig*, although he only once appeared in the office in his swimming trunks!

Seahorse... He was Australian with a somewhat singular character like the *seahorse* and could turn his hands to most things needed in the business.

Live, Love, Teach... By now I was running Intuitive Vision Board workshops with some frequency and attracting mostly women.

Flowers... I was starting to bloom again, as I helped other people's lives to flourish.

02: Invocation

03: Invention

04: Inception

05: Immersion

06: Illumination

07: Integration

08: Inauguration

Yoga teacher... I observed how Tao Porchon-Lynch's Lotus pose connected her to Remarkable-Right brain by opening up her left-hand (heart) side, as her arm reached for the heavens, while she sat grounded, cross-legged, with her right hand touching the earth. What a suitable metaphor for the Intuitive Vision Board journey I was undertaking and encouraging others to do the same by attending my workshop.

Did making the Intuitive Vision Board provide me with hope, vitality and inspiration? Absolutely yes!

Did it help me to source work that was right up my street, which I'd never heard of before? Definitely yes!

Did it unlock my creativity and find a fresh outlet for it? Very much so!

Six years later...

If money is the only measure of success then as I write this book I don't rank up there with American investor Warren Buffett, one of the richest people on earth. Even so, my progress has been considerable. It's healthy for me to acknowledge the milestones I have reached, as it will be for you to record the distance you travel along your path and how your Intuitive Vision Board has enabled you to redefine your personal lifescape.

Practicalities addressed ~ *Milestone 1*

I fed, clothed and housed us adequately on my own. I bought a small car and enough furniture and chattels to equip a small home. I was fit and well, and I was not addicted to anything.

Foundations for the future ~ *Milestone 2*

After a bumpy start, my daughter sailed through her "A" level years, able to go to her university of choice (Bristol), to study her favourite subject (History) and emerge with a First Class honours degree.

Manifested a windfall ~ *Milestone 3*

By applying my Feng Shui expertise in one of the properties we rented, I manifested a windfall of £35,000. This enabled me to suspend the part-time job for six months and concentrate on my own business and create a website. I could also afford some part-time help to provide the skills I didn't have.

Career success ~ *Milestone 4*

Once through the initial challenges, I ran innumerable Intuitive Vision Board workshops and provided coaching and Feng Shui consultations. I hosted four week-long Soul Alive Retreats in Istria, Croatia, the Algarve, and the Tarn Valley in France. I was doing my thing.

Became a published author ~ *Milestone 5*

My desire to write this book emerged quietly as I entered the third year of resurrection from the ashes. I was able to raise a loan to afford to do so, which three years previously would have been impossible. It took me the span of two and a half years and latterly I returned to full-time employment in a solicitor's practice, which kept the money coming in, while I wrote during the weekends and holidays.

Altogether these milestones feel like a huge achievement and I'm absolutely thrilled you are reading this book.

Here you are now at the end of Chapter 1 – Initiation. I hope you have enjoyed reading my story about how the Intuitive Vision Board found a way through complexity when my LL-brain had given up hope. I also trust you can see how this initiation – and my embracing it – actually was the ripening of me. Above all I'd like to think you are encouraged and not dissuaded from starting out on your own odyssey, with the opportunity for personal transformation it beholds. Sometimes you need to be prepared to venture into a darker place before you are ready to move out again into the light, with velocity. So don't be afraid to confront whatever it is that may be troubling you or blocking your way. The pain of not doing so, or putting off making changes until later, is often greater than taking action when it is due, as my own story illustrates.

In Chapter 2 – Invocation – we take a closer look at the unique qualities of the Intuitive Vision Board that make it stand out from other manifestation techniques. In the meantime, I wish you a fascinating and inspirational adventure and look forward to seeing you on the other side.

02: Invocation

03: Invention

04: Inception

05: Immersion

06: Illumination

07: Integration

08: Inauguration

02: Invocation

03: Invention

04: Inception

05: Immersion

06: Illumination

07: Integration

08: Inauguration

"And then the day came when the risk to remain tight inside the bud was greater than the risk to blossom."

Anaïs Nin, Novelist

Chapter 2

INVOCATION

Change

When you've touched the bottom and the repercussions are still swirling around your feet, you'll be very keen to find an exit strategy. Any pain or discomfort – physical or emotional – provides a strong motivation to make changes to alleviate both. However, your circumstances don't need to be extreme to warrant making an Intuitive Vision Board. You might just have come to a temporary standstill and have no vision as to what you might do next and you can't conjure one up out of thin air.

Most people who have attended my workshop are seeking one or more of these six outcomes:

> » **Clarity** over the options
> » **Focus** on the right things
> » **Creativity** to do something different
> » **Confidence** to trust in themselves
> » **Courage** to embrace change
> » **Guidance** as to which step to take next

You too may welcome help in locating your True North. But in the absence of something – or someone –to jolt you off your current trajectory, the temptation is to bumble along, staying comfortably in the known-zone and avoiding the risk to blossom. The insights revealed by the Intuitive Vision Board may be just the encouraging jolt you need. Superficially it appears to be a collage of colourful images. But when you plumb its depths, it broadcasts the real aspirations and untapped potential of its maker that can too quickly get drowned out in the noisy throng of everyday life. Such as:

> » Who you *really* are off duty
> » Who you *desire* to become
> » What you *truly* value in life
> » What you'd *love* to do more of
> » Places *enticing* you to visit
> » Activities *calling out* for you to try
> » People to *spend* more time with
> » *Finding* purpose to your life

There are other names used to describe this non-artistic collage – a mood board, a dream board, and a manifestation board are among them. Vision boards are certainly a phenomenon of our times, made famous by celebrities like Oprah Winfrey, and are particularly popular on her side of the Atlantic. But not all vision boards are alike because of the way in which they are created. Most of them begin with the end in mind and find words and pictures to reflect this. *This is planning not visioning.* The Intuitive Vision Board doesn't do this and therefore stands in a class of its own as being truly visionary.

Visionary

Dictionary definitions of "visionary" include:

inspired, imaginative, creative, inventive, insightful, ingenious, enterprising, innovative, perceptive, intuitive, farsighted.

All of these marvellously emotive words excite me and are precisely the qualities you need to draw upon when you've run out of steam or are facing hurdles that seem insurmountable. The Intuitive Vision Board helps you to locate these visionary qualities in yourself. It enables you to see beyond the obvious as to what the next best and most evolutionary steps for you might be. It helps you entertain possibilities over and above the ideas you have of yourself – and others have of you, beyond their more limited but well-meaning perspective.

The words "vision" and "visionary" predate the invention of vision boards, however. There was Moses, for example, who received his assignment from God in the burning bush, while a female exponent was Joan of Arc, who took counsel from her frequent visions in her assignment to free France from the English. The common denominators in both these historic examples are worth noting: the visionaries weren't seeking a vision; they were sought to execute one. Certainly they were open to the possibility but they did not know in advance of receiving it what it might constitute; the vision was revealed to them along with implicit instructions on how to put it together. Moreover, the scope of their visions extended way beyond their existing conceptual framework of what they thought they *should* be doing and as a consequence changed the course of their lives – and the lives of many others too – *forever.*

When we look behind the scenes at most contemporary vision boards, the visions are a lot tamer in comparison and less ground-breaking than those received by Moses or Joan of Arc. Why is that? Because their scope is limited to images chosen by their maker to meet predetermined definitions of what success and happiness should look like. This is always only from the finite frame of reference of Logical-Left and the limited pool of information already stored inside the maker's cognitive mind. This type of concept board originated in the world of design, where it served to capture ideas, moods and

01: Initiation

02: Invocation

03: Invention

04: Inception

05: Immersion

06: Illumination

07: Integration

08: Inauguration

01: Initiation

02: Invocation

03: Invention

04: Inception

05: Immersion

06: Illumination

07: Integration

08: Inauguration

concepts together in one place on a particular subject. From the outset the designer is deliberately working to a brief and controlling the search filters to meet it.

Entitlement

When Logical-Left brain is the driving force behind the vision board, in all probability it will become an illustrated wish-list, conjured up by the ego. There is no room for surprises, because you've already determined what it is you are looking for and are seeking pictures to fit this view. If you're the kind of person who knows exactly what they want and likes to be in control, making a vision board in this way will appeal to you. However, there is an underlying premise to this approach, which is worth exposing. It is that you are entitled to have whatever you want, once you've decided what it is, visualised it on your vision board, and focused on it frequently enough to manifest it. This is not a vision in the original and mystical sense of the word. This is willpower.

If everyone were to make a vision board with this motivation, it would be a bit like saying to a group of children outside a sweet shop: "You can have whatever you like, darlings" – and then leaving them to get on with it. The likelihood is that the more dominant, determined children will be in there first and consume more than they need. Some children may get trodden on in the rush. Some may not get into the shop at all and are left outside in tears with resentment brewing. In the ensuing chaos, the shop is trashed and there are no sweets left for another time. For me this is a microcosm of the behaviour we witness on the global stage. And the entitlement approach to making a vision board perpetuates this because it implies you can have any sweets you want, at any time, and can help yourself to them. The winner takes all and there is mindless overconsumption of shared resources, irrespective of the consequences for the rest of humanity, other life forms, or the planet itself.

Respect

This approach to visioning leaves me cold as you've probably guessed already. It's greedy and immature and ironically lacks any real vision. It speaks mostly about acquisition for "me" and "mine", as opposed to what I am able to give to the best of my abilities and how I can offer my resources, in collaboration with others, so everyone benefits. Entitlement lacks foresight or any desire to leave a legacy for our children, let alone other people's children or for future generations. This noble sentiment disappeared with the Edwardians – except perhaps in Denmark.

29

01: Initiation

02: Invocation

03: Invention

04: Inception

05: Immersion

06: Illumination

07: Integration

08: Inauguration

The Danes are reputedly and repeatedly the happiest people on earth according to World Happiness Report rankings, where even the poorest enjoy a high standard of living. Whether the Danes are born smarter, possibly their country is small enough for them to still experience themselves as one tribe and to look out for one another, or perhaps self-seeking behaviour is not part of their cultural make-up. Whatever it is, their collective behaviour is intelligent. And it's shocking how far behind Denmark the attitude of the rest of the world trails, except in perhaps other Scandinavian countries.

The Danes' wise, egalitarian attitude permeates their entire society and they won't tolerate any one person dominating things for too long. They maintain a staunch belief in fostering the rights of the individual to enjoy a decent life. At the same time they have the wit to realise this will require them all to contribute exceptionally high taxes, particularly those who are better off. In addition each individual is accountable for making a substantial social and environmental contribution to their society. I can't help but say, respect, respect.

Money can't buy it

There is one big, glaring obstacle, however, in tossing out the entitlement approach to vision boards in favour of the intuitive kind and that is it can get results. Back in the mid-80s, I wasn't making vision boards. I was, however, firmly in the grip of the entitlement mentality behind entitlement vision boards when my partner and I formed a marketing agency, which served Fortune 500 companies. It was driven by our egos, because at the time we didn't know any better – and thankfully our egos weren't that big. As marketing director, I was intentional in cherry-picking the corporates I wanted as clients and pursuing them until they were. I lived in a beautiful home created with an interior designer. I drove an expensive BMW. I shopped for clothes in Milan. I had three foreign holidays a year. If I'd known to create a vision board back then, a self-indulgent wish-list would have appeared on my wall.

This wilful mentality also has its downside, as does the entitlement vision board. That is, you can suddenly and unexpectedly run out of steam, because the vision you are pursing is neither organic nor part of a bigger picture that is in the interests of everybody. Six years into the agency, I became disillusioned and bored and began to have panic attacks. My lifestyle was deluxe but I worked 5½ days a week, 12 hours a day, to maintain it. It brought me material trappings but very little sense of connection and fulfilment. Nor did it furnish my life with deeper meaning and purpose.

Everywhere I looked in the business world at that time I saw avarice and competition driving corporate behaviour and I felt a lack of integrity that our marketing agency was

01: Initiation

02: Invocation

03: Invention

04: Inception

05: Immersion

06: Illumination

07: Integration

08: Inauguration

contributing to this. What did I do about it? I sold my share of the business. I didn't know what I would do next or how to go about discovering what that was and so I dabbled and experimented. I sourced Native American arts from Arizona and New Mexico and opened a gallery. The Intuitive Vision Board would have been the perfect tool for me – but I hadn't invented it back then. I spent another two years of trial and error before retraining in a profession in which I felt I could add more lasting value: Feng Shui – the art of living mindfully by creating vibrant and harmonious living and working spaces. And I have been in practice ever since.

Ancient wisdom

My confusion back then as marketing director, which is still evident in the majority of entitlement vision boards on the scene today, hinges around the word "vision". Is it truly a vision or is it a goal-setting exercise using pictures? And what happens when your deep, individual values conflict with the predominant cultural paradigm of success? From my observations, typically your values are usurped in favour of ladder-climbing and material advancement, while your personal and romantic life languishes in the wake if this continues unattended.

Perhaps there is something to be gleaned from two older civilisations. Both regarded the vision as a visitation from a higher intelligence beyond the self. According to Native American tradition, when a person lost their way in life they went on a vision quest. They removed themselves from the tribe to live a solitary existence, to fast and to connect closely with nature – all in preparation for the moment when the spiritual guidance they sought would be forthcoming to inspire the next stage of their life.

In Ancient Greece, they too believed a vision came from the Gods. They had a different approach to creating the ideal conditions for receiving this, which is somewhat aligned with our current notions of taking a retreat. When someone was on the brink of depression, boredom or burnout, friends and family encouraged them to head for the sacred temple of Asclepius. Here resided the deity associated with healing and medicine, whose symbol (the serpent-intertwined rod) is still associated with medicine and health care today. While on retreat, the initiate bathed, rested, ate nourishing food, enjoyed music, the arts, dance, drama, and received healing – all with the purpose of entering a different state of consciousness, increasing their receptivity, and invoking the portents from a divine source. In the meantime, the initiate waited... and they waited... until one

31

01: Initiation

02: Invocation

03: Invention

04: Inception

05: Immersion

06: Illumination

07: Integration

08: Inauguration

night in the temple of Asclepius the visitation was revealed in the form of a dream that would herald the way forward and provide a greater context for their life.

Carolyn Myss, author of *The Anatomy of the Spirit*, generally describes this type of visitation as awakening to your divine potential in order to fulfil your sacred contract. The success of the mission depends on your willingness to surrender *your* will to God's will, totality or universal intelligence, whichever makes most sense to you. This then returns us full circle to the difference between the entitlement vision *you decide* upon, which will require considerable willpower to pull off, and the unpremeditated vision *you receive*, which has been assigned to you with the full force of the universe flowing through it. Which one do you fancy?

From ambition to inspiration

My experience of facilitating the Intuitive Vision Board workshop has shown me that the majority of people who show up don't know what their vision is, what they are looking for and therefore what should be on their vision board. Often they feel guilty about this, as if they should know. In light of what's been said earlier, hooray! Their hesitancy is a welcome relief. It means their ego is not permanently positioned in the driving seat and they are more receptive to becoming a human conduit for a visionary assignment and the guidance to go with it. Should they happen to express a preference as to what things they'd like to see on their Intuitive Vision Board, they are wise enough not to be too attached to this or insist on having things work out their way. Ideas change during the creative session and evolve over the coming weeks, which is to be expected since life itself is organic, unpredictable and changeable.

Prior to attending the Intuitive Vision Board workshop I seek to understand where everyone is coming from and what they hope to gain from it. Over the years this amounts to a lot of people so I can confidently give you the most common reasons people report for making the Intuitive Vision Board. You may recognise yourself among them:

> » "I don't have a vision and I feel I should have one."
> » "I'm busy but I don't feel I'm focused on the right things."
> » "I need to make an important decision and I can't decide."
> » "I don't know what it is I truly want or need."
> » "Money is not a problem but absence of fulfilment is."
> » "I'd like to know what my higher purpose is."
> » "I've been ill and I'm taking time to evaluate my life choices."

01: Initiation

02: Invocation

03: Invention

04: Inception

05: Immersion

06: Illumination

07: Integration

08: Inauguration

How then to awaken your intuition and make the shift from ego-driven visioning to *heart-led visionary* in making the Intuitive Vision Board?

The first requirement is to interrupt the incessant chatter of the Logical-Left egoic mind, mentioned in Chapter 1, along with its conditioned thinking and preconceived notions of what's right for you. You can't make a vision board intuitively with that rattling off in your ear. You want to be free to wander where you like into pastures new and Logical-Left will be very unhappy about this. Its role is to keep you safe and that means away from any changes to your life circumstances because it's a big fan of the status quo.

Remarkable-Right brain will want you instead to start out with an empty mind, to be open to mystery, and willing to entertain surprises. You will need also to park any pre-existing attachment to believing it will require determination and willpower to enforce your vision. It is perhaps for this reason I had to wait a further two years, following my departure from the marketing agency. I needed time to thaw out enough mentally and put sufficient distance between me and the materialistic paradigm, to be able to explore the next stage of my life differently and wisely.

New-age thinking would have us believe we alone determine our destiny. It's not very fashionable to think like an Ancient Greek and be comfortable seeking guidance from the non-physical realm. But this prejudice has to change now in order to accommodate a much wider field of possibilities. It's time for us each to assume our special assignments and in so doing become the life-affirming visionaries we are all capable of becoming. But we can't do this while we remain stuck in a linear groove and insist on being in charge. If we continue, our egos rampantly doing their own greedy thing will surely wipe us out – within 100 years, according to Eckhart Tolle, spiritual teacher of worldwide renown and author of the bestseller *The Power of Now*.

Transmission

The Intuitive Vision Board is an important and accessible tool for tuning into your intuition and dialoguing with the higher intelligence that can – and wants to – collaborate with you.

The process is a creative meditation, a form of art therapy, and a spiritual conversation that arises out of stillness. Territory that was previously unexplored and unavailable to you now opens up new vistas. By making the Intuitive Vision Board you forge a relationship between what previously seemed to be disparate and unrelated subjects. In so doing you make bold leaps of the imagination, cross boundaries and create new paradigms.

The constellation of images that appear before you on the Intuitive Vision Board is a narrative that arises quite spontaneously, yet the finished product displays an inherent order without your control or command. This is emergence in action and is quite extraordinary. It's as though the images select *you* (rather than you selecting them) and over time they show you why it is they belong together and what this can yield.

You will seldom see literal goals represented on the board in the way the ego would have chosen them; instead the images point towards the target but they are not the actual target. They are symbols and metaphors – openings to deeper layers of interpretation, whose purpose and significance will grow clearer over time. They build a bridge between your deepest desires and the widest purpose the universe has for you.

You may find there are images appearing serendipitously on your Intuitive Vision Board, which you may well have chosen for yourself if I'd encouraged you to hunt for them. However, what you'll more likely find is that these images have a nuance of meaning beyond your first interpretation. You will also discover the hidden links on your board that ignite the whole and stitch the vision together in a way that is pure genius.

A potential future is mapped out on your Intuitive Vision Board, which often includes the next steps and the order in which they are to be taken. The curious thing is this won't become apparent to your cognitive Logical-Left until *after* you are living the vision – and only on reflection. It's as though an exterior, invisible force is propelling you along in the interim. Here's an example of this in action.

How an intuitive vision transforms a family's situation

Arabella is a passionate woman with considerable energy; however, when I first spoke to her she felt stuck in a rut. "I feel I've got a ball and chain attached to me," she said. "I'm hoping the vision board will uncover the solution."

03: Invention

04: Inception

05: Immersion

06: Illumination

07: Integration

08: Inauguration

01: Initiation

02: Invocation

03: Invention

04: Inception

05: Immersion

06: Illumination

07: Integration

08: Inauguration

Here are some of the things that were troubling them. Any one of these alone would have slowed them down but taken altogether, they amounted to an elephantine roadblock in their eyes.

» Their greenbelt home was under threat of 750 homes being built over their back fence and already house prices were plummeting. They wanted to sell but didn't know how in this climate.

» Her husband was groaning his way through a three-hour daily commute for the money in a job he'd outgrown and was in need of a *big* holiday.

» Their three-year-old needed lots of attention and there was no time for Arabella to develop an additional income stream, while her exhausted husband had little energy for family life.

» Letting their flat in London would have eased the financial strain but it had sat empty for six months.

» Their small car was cramped, aging fast, and not equipped for a young family and a dog.

» There was no support coming from either grandparent and no spare cash for childcare.

Six months after making her Intuitive Vision Board, absolutely *everything* about their lives changed for the better – none of it planned or scheduled beforehand. At first nothing seemed to be moving. It later transpired that all the signs were indicated on Arabella's very busy vision board, every available inch covered with carefully arranged images. Here are the highlights of their transformation.

The very same evening as the terrorist bomb at the Ariana Grande concert in Manchester, when everyone was mourning the tragedy, Arabella's husband was returning home from a dog walk at 11pm. A drunken driver ran into the row of parked cars outside their house, inflicting his "local terror' with such force that he wrote off two cars (including Arabella's and a van) while her husband's Mini had to be sent away for serious repairs. Both dog and husband were fortunate not to be killed. Now, without means of transport, the couple seized the moment to purchase a new family car, which turned out to be near in shape and colour to the one on her vision board. The wheels were in motion...

35

01: Initiation

02: Invocation

03: Invention

04: Inception

05: Immersion

06: Illumination

07: Integration

08: Inauguration

With the family car now ready to go, they began speculating on a holiday – a grand tour of the UK. Then suddenly, the husband was made redundant and received a more than decent pay-off. Declining another job in the same company, he made straight for the exit and the lure of a new career. Now with car, money and time on their hands, the UK tour morphed into a massive European road trip, which the husband, the strategist, set about planning with pleasure.

Since they would now be away longer than the original three weeks, they decided to rent out their house for three months and called in an estate agent to take photos. He knew they'd been interested in selling and had given up, so he suggested they took the opportunity to also put their house up for sale and see what happened. Two weeks into their holiday, their house sold!

Meanwhile, what a road trip it was. Through France, Belgium, Germany, Switzerland, Croatia, Slovenia, Italy, Monaco, Monte Carlo, Cote d'Azur, and Spain with a little help from an airline since Spain is such a huge country. Never more than a four-hour drive each day, averaging two to four-night stopovers, booking accommodation as they went. Their son was no trouble at all and loved every minute of it.

Everywhere they went, Arabella remembered images similar to those on her vision board – and ones she'd forgotten, but spotted on her return – waterfalls, glowing orange sunsets, beaches, small white buildings, everywhere forests displaying the autumn colours. One bedroom even had butterfly stencils reminiscent of the ones on her board, while in Venice the Murano glass reminded her of the coloured glass lampshades she'd carefully cut out and pasted down.

Back home, Arabella spotted the words *make a move* on her board right underneath *Ryanair* – the very same airline they'd used to get them across Spain – and both sitting right alongside images of a passport and jubilant woman with her arms outstretched. I wonder who that represented?

But where were they going to live now on their return? Arabella's husband had been scanning the rental listings during the roadtrip, particularly those by the sea – which isn't surprising since the word *coast* was emblazoned right across the middle of his wife's vision board. He was particularly drawn to a small town in Devon, 15 minutes' drive away from work opportunities in Plymouth, but unfortunately the house was already taken.

On their return home, however, the very same property came back on the market. They fast-tracked to Devon, snapped up the rental and the very next day had

01: Initiation

02: Invocation

03: Invention

04: Inception

05: Immersion

06: Illumination

07: Integration

08: Inauguration

their son's name down for a pre-school and primary school, both with *outstanding* Ofsted reports, in the same small town.

Meanwhile, they found tenants for their rental flat in London, which in time they will sell to finance the home they will eventually purchase in Devon. As for the unsupportive grandparents... one died in this same period and the other misbehaved so badly that contact has been severed completely.

Congratulations to them both for a remarkable turnaround. Arabella had the vision, but her husband got right behind her in responding to it. Each one of those shackles, binding them to the ball and chain, had been cut loose, thanks to a little help from the Intuitive Vision Board. The steering was there and they had the courage to grab the wheel and go with it.

Moved to tears

In my workshops it's not unusual to see people moved to tears, as they recall parts of themselves and buried dreams that have been dismissed to toe the party line. The problem is that when you conform to external pressure, it can dampen your spiritual nature too and your connection to deeper wisdom. Then you cannot know what living with authenticity is or what you'd give your wholehearted *yes* to. It's not possible to entertain living your visionary purpose when this is the case. No wonder there are tears, which if unaddressed can develop into symptoms of depression to mask the chasm.

I once ran the Intuitive Vision Board workshop for 12 CEOs of small to medium-size companies. There were nine men and three women, all members of an executive club, and this workshop formed part of their annual retreat. The organiser had briefed me beforehand about each person's circumstance. They also requested me to focus the visioning process on business and not on personal aspirations because this was felt to be more important to CEOs. I smiled to myself on hearing this. Ultimately CEOs are human like the rest of us and whatever pulled at their heart and was genuinely significant to them would surely appear on their Intuitive Vision Board, whether it was related to business or not. It was not for me to send them in a particular direction but to trust the creative process to deliver what they most needed to hear and to show what adjustments they could make to keep them healthy, sane and inspired. This, more than anything, would support and enhance their leadership ability.

37

01: Initiation

02: Invocation

03: Invention

04: Inception

05: Immersion

06: Illumination

07: Integration

08: Inauguration

We'd got to the stage in the creative inquiry where people were putting the finishing touches on their vision boards and I was doing a final sweep of the room to see what had emerged. I approached a man I'd been told had a very successful software company. Middle-aged and overweight, he was unhappy and, in spite of monthly coaching, had not got to the bottom of it. What caught my attention on his board was the large photograph of two Argentine tango dancers in the centre. Astonished, I blurted out the obvious: "they're tango dancers in close embrace", at which point I glanced across at the CEO and saw tears in his eyes. "Yes," he said, "not only was I a very good tango dancer once, I was also a good teacher. I'm such a long way removed from this now and it's hurting. I must do something about it."

What had happened for him is not untypical. There is a tendency to push aside hobbies and pastimes in favour of activities we consider should have greater priority. But often the former is the very oil we need to lubricate our wheels. The fact it shows up on the Intuitive Vision Board is a clear indication the maker must find a way to incorporate this into their life – or ignore it at their peril.

I have never seen anyone walk away disappointed with their Intuitive Vision Board. On the contrary, midway through the workshop I witness people who are totally engaged in creative activity, not anxiously looking over their shoulders to compare their vision board with their neighbour's. At this point I am the one who is moved to tears as I give thanks for the privilege of helping to midwife the visions now emerging and witnessing the profound shifts that are occurring.

What fascinates me over time is the degree of constancy that appears on the vision boards of returning creators (because I encourage you to make a new board roughly every year). Images may bear resemblance from board to board but they are never identical, each re-occurrence unveiling a different aspect of the theme. This makes me wonder if the content of the Intuitive Vision Board is less about what the creator needs to be happy and more about what they need to stay aligned to their true calling – a theme which is likely to have travelled with them a whole lifetime.

01: Initiation

02: Invocation

03: Invention

04: Inception

05: Immersion

06: Illumination

07: Integration

08: Inauguration

Hidden treasure

The journey you're about to undertake in making the Intuitive Vision Board has an additional pay-off. You are going to discover diamonds. The only catch is you are unlikely to recognise them as diamonds immediately, so you'll have to take my word for it: they are hidden on your board. If I'd known this at the start of my heroine's journey, I might have relaxed more and fretted less. I would have trusted more readily that somehow things would turn out for the best and fretted less that I would be left penniless on the streets. If you're currently in the middle of a transition, please don't make it worse for yourself by insisting you ought to have a better attitude. Acknowledge the attitude you have – and any feelings which accompany it – then get right on down to making your Intuitive Vision Board. Your Logical-Left brain may still attempt to persuade you that you ought to be doing something more productive. Ignore it – and hang in there until your board is complete.

This journey is also an invocation in which you are as much the investigated as the investigator. Remembering this will help you to stay open and curious and not feel like you need to be in control all of the time. It also helps if you remember not to take any of life's challenges personally. You have not failed. You are not doomed for eternity. Both of which had crossed my mind at the time. You may even surprise yourself by finding the very situation you are working through becomes the gift you eventually give back to the world as you discover diamonds in the most unlikely of places, which this next story demonstrates.

39

01: Initiation

02: Invocation

03: Invention

04: Inception

05: Immersion

06: Illumination

07: Integration

08: Inauguration

Acres of diamonds

There are many versions of this story, but I like the one told by Russell Conwell. He was a visionary and an educational entrepreneur, who delivered his speech over 6000 times around the world to raise money to create Temple University, USA. He believed the pathway to personal success was largely through education; that educated people were in turn obliged to help the less fortunate to realise their full potential and it was the duty of everyone to meet the needs of their community. This sounds rather like the Danish worldview I described earlier; how delightful is that.

Conwell's tale, succinctly told here, was about a man from Persia called Al Hafed. He wanted to find diamonds so badly he left his family, sold his property and set off in a futile search for them which ultimately killed him. Meanwhile, the new owner of his old home discovered a rich diamond mine located right underneath the very property Al Hafed had deserted. Not surprisingly, the new owner lived happily ever after in it.

Acres of diamonds is a reminder that when you go hunting for success, which has been defined by greed and not by the heart, the motivation is not coming from deep within you. The big dream doesn't quite hang together; there's plenty enough to live on but not enough to live for. Meanwhile, we can overlook the diamonds right under our noses – which are buried within ourselves – because we are too preoccupied in believing we need to look for them in foreign lands.

This is what can happen when Logical-Left takes charge of making a vision board. Steering you towards things it believes should make you happy, you can overlook the obvious. I remember once leading a workshop with another group of CEOs and at the end of the creative process one of them piped up: "I don't believe it! This board is showing me I have absolutely everything I could want and need already but I hadn't appreciated it until now. Why am I working so hard? Why am I still striving?" The Intuitive Vision Board will always include any diamonds you already have that may just need polishing up, as well as those buried, waiting to be discovered.

And since we have been talking about uncovering treasure, let's end this chapter with a short story about a windfall.

Intuitive vision strikes gold

Penelope struck lucky with the first Intuitive Vision Board she made with me. Without an intention in mind, she'd cut out a piece of gold foil, which had circular patterns on it resembling gold coins. Four weeks later she received an envelope in the post from the People's Postcode Lottery. It contained a strip of foil with an uncanny resemblance to the one on her vision board. She discovered she'd won £5,800 – while Penelope's son was thrilled to receive his first car for Christmas as a consequence, all thanks to the piece of gold foil.

Let's roll on to Chapter 3 – Invention – and how making the Intuitive Vision Board serves to awaken the genius within.

01: Initiation

02: Invocation

03: Invention

04: Inception

05: Immersion

06: Illumination

07: Integration

08: Inauguration

"Who looks outside dreams; who looks inside awakes."

Carl Jung, Psychoanalyst

01: Initiation

02: Invocation

03: Invention

04: Inception

05: Immersion

06: Illumination

07: Integration

08: Inauguration

Chapter 3

INVENTION

01: Initiation

02: Invocation

03: Invention

04: Inception

05: Immersion

06: Illumination

07: Integration

08: Inauguration

Aha!

The blinding flash... the stroke of genius... the epiphany... the defining moment... Eureka! All of these describe so eloquently the moment when the answer to something you pondered over arrives unexpectedly. Aha!

You might expect this to happen to inventors like Mozart and Einstein and conclude that creative breakthrough is the prerogative of the gifted few. Not so. Admittedly not everyone is destined to compose a symphony or invent new technology. But you too have the capacity for bold, innovative thinking so long as you don't expect your genius to be delivered in a tidy package with a timed delivery. Sometimes it is, mostly it isn't. However, you have more control over the conditions that encourage creative thinking than you might first imagine. You can be an agent for change in the circles in which you orbit on matters you are passionate about and perhaps ignoring. Wouldn't that be handy to remember when you are wondering what to do next and are left treading water?

As I mentioned earlier, you have more brain capacity to draw on in these matters than you might think. I've used the words "Remarkable-Right brain" and "Logical-Left brain" throughout to distinguish between the two capacities – the former is inclined towards intuition and the latter towards intellect. And yet these two capacities are as much metaphors as specific locations in the brain. In the grand design of things no-one was excluded from having both, although some are more endowed towards one side of the brain than the other. The significance of having both is that you are able to access two different states of consciousness with the ability to move seamlessly between the two, when you learn how and choose to exercise this prerogative. We'll see later how the Intuitive Vision Board facilitates this.

In the meantime unless you've slipped through the net as an artist or poet, your education will have favoured Logical-Left brain development. Therefore our society and culture is mostly the result of logical, sequential, causal reasoning. Logical-Left is the more active, masculine energy. It likes process thinking and concerns itself with how to manipulate our physical reality. The more receptive feminine energy is represented by Remarkable-Right. It is unlikely you have received any formal education in how to cultivate illogical, non-linear, out-of-the-box thinking, which is not governed by cause and effect. Yet in a Remarkable-Right frame of mind, ideas and information are sourced from a different realm entirely – the collective unconscious, the unmanifest realm, pure potentiality. And in ignoring this faculty, the potential for a creative breakthrough or to become a visionary in your own lifetime is zero.

43

01: Initiation

02: Invocation

03: Invention

04: Inception

05: Immersion

06: Illumination

07: Integration

08: Inauguration

Brainy

Wait a minute. How do I know the concept of Logical-Left and Remarkable-Right isn't all in the mind anyway? Well yes, it is to do with the mind – but not entirely. And no, you are not imagining it. It's not possible to pin down exactly where our intelligence resides and where ideas and information originate from. Evidence suggests that consciousness exists independently of brain activity as when people have a near-death experience. On their return to life, they are able to relate the events which occurred even when their brain-wave activity measured flat. The differentiation between Remarkable-Right and Logical-Left has more to do with how we think than what we think about.

Their appearance is different too. When you slice through the left brain you discover white matter very tightly packed, in a linear fashion with defined pathways. A slice through the right brain is quite the opposite. The white matter is far less dense and the neurones are broader, branching out in a slow meandering fashion, rather like a mature river valley. The flashes of insight that precede an Aha! moment are accompanied by a large burst of neural activity in the Remarkable-Right hemisphere. You would witness this occurring, especially towards the end of the Intuitive Vision Board workshop, if I had people wired up during the session.

Neuroscience defines three types of thinking, which loosely correspond to the two halves of the brain.

1. The first is *convergent* which employs the Logical-Left hemisphere exclusively.
2. The middle ground is occupied by *divergent* thinking, which draws on both Logical-Left and Remarkable-Right hemispheres in that order.
3. The third is *emergent* thinking which employs the Remarkable-Right hemisphere entirely.

1. Convergent

You will never arrive at those elusive Aha! moments by churning the Logical-Left harder over a pre-defined set of options to achieve a breakthrough. This is not how Mozart sourced his genius and it won't be for you. This reduces the playing field even before the game has started, eliminating the possibility of innovation and rendering real creativity powerless. *Convergent thinking* has its strengths but in the context of visions and creativity, it does not. To think like a visionary we must find a way to engage Remarkable-

Right while distracting Logical-Left, which we touched upon earlier. Otherwise Logical-Left will act like a gatekeeper, determining what is acceptable to let in and what must stay out.

2. Divergent

To cultivate creative thinking, we must widen the field to get beyond what is known and normal, and encourage so-called *divergent thinking*. Judgement is deferred while we open up to as many possibilities in a non-linear manner, then fish for the best answer from this expanded pool. Ideas find their way into the net that normally wouldn't make it. The divergent approach is better for creativity but it is still too limiting for a visionary because the issue to be explored has already been predetermined. It puts convergent and divergent thinking at either ends of the same continuum, both defined by each other.

3. Emergent

The third possibility, *emergent thinking*, is truly visionary. Still in its early days of application, there have been various attempts at its definition. To my mind what distinguishes emergent thinking from the other two is that there is *no* brief, no declaration of what the issue or problem is at the outset. The field emerges and the possibilities come into view by venturing one step at a time into virgin territory. Sir Ken Robinson, the well-known advisor on creativity in education, expressed this well when he said: "There isn't a path – you create your path as you take it. It emerges as you walk along it."

In philosophy, systems theory, and art, emergence occurs when "the whole proves to be greater than the sum of the parts". In terms of the Intuitive Vision Board this means the entirety of the board has potential and properties which the individual images treated in isolation do not have. These properties emerge because of the manner in which the images interact with one another and because of their place within the whole. All this achieved not by planning but by allowing the pieces to fall into place.

So thumbs up to those of us who are courageous enough to promote Remarkable-Right and emergent thinking – and you, the creator of the Intuitive Vision Board, are among them. Society has fixated on the supremacy of Logical-Left and convergent thinking for too long and produced what have been described as backwards evolutionary tendencies. For instance, the annihilation of the human species and its habitation: since recorded history, it is estimated one billion people have been killed by war and genocide due to our collective Logical-Left brain madness, while the elevation and advancement of digital technology, perpetuated by Logical-Left, has further served to increase the rift between the two brain hemispheres. The time has come to restore balance between the two and explore how each of us can ride on the coat-tails of Remarkable-Right and emergent thinking, if we are to transform business, education and our communities for the better.

Light bulb moments

There have been times when I've flowed with creativity and welcomed a few Aha! moments in my life. I'm sure you have too. The one most pertinent to the Intuitive Vision Board process came while I was studying Somatic Arts Psychotherapy. The Aha! didn't occur while I was immersed in Logical-Left brain essay writing or referencing a stack of books in preparation. It arrived quietly while I was out walking the dog, my Logical-Left switched off, and my Remarkable-Right doing nothing in particular but enjoying the beauty of nature.

I'd been pondering how to bring the wisdom of the Master's degree to a much wider audience, beyond those actively engaged in therapy or counselling. During my studies we'd experienced a variety of ways to awaken the Remarkable-Right and foster emergent thinking through the expressive arts, which Jung called *active imagination*. We learned how to engage Remarkable-Right in dialogue with the collective unconscious and pure potentiality through creative self-expression: activities such as movement, art, writing, making, sounding – all the while remaining alert and present to what was emerging but never attempting to control or influence it. Besides, it was understood that the choice is always yours whether to engage with the information that comes streaming through; it's not as if an idea is about to take you over against your will.

It's thanks to Carl Jung's genius that *active imagination* is now accepted practice. His visionary breakthrough inspired a whole generation of educators to apply this practice in many different contexts. Such spontaneous, improvised thinking scares the pants off Logical-Left who likes to build on what is known already. Logical-Left will proclaim these creative activities to be fun but to have no intellectual value whatsoever. Reflect back over the times in your life when the germ of an idea or inspiration occurred to you and was squashed, even before you had a chance to explore it further.

01: Initiation

02: Invocation

03: Invention

04: Inception

05: Immersion

06: Illumination

07: Integration

08: Inauguration

Into the woods

Incidentally, Carl Jung's breakthrough with active imagination occurred while he was going through a dark night of the soul following the break-up of his relationship with close friend and mentor, Sigmund Freud. For the best part of two years he struggled, lost and directionless. The story goes that in the mornings he continued with his psychiatric clinic. Some genius persuaded him to take the afternoons off and prompted him to return to a childhood pastime, which had brought him much joy: to make model houses out of wood. Not only did this allow him to come to terms with this painful transition but it also uncovered his professional pathway ahead. Jung's breakthrough didn't occur by actively dwelling on his problem, while he was busy in his clinic. The urge to return to wood-crafting occurred while he was out in nature. He began it without purpose. He just played. And the impulse to continue lasted for several years and was quickly accompanied by other modes of engaging the active imagination through creative expression.

Please note, it was *not* the finished product that transformed Jung's personal and professional life; it was the very process itself – creating, mulling and moulding with his hands – that did it. After two years he'd worked through this depressive period and birthed an entirely new approach to psychotherapy: the active imagination. Aha!

Answer to prayers

While I found all the various ways of engaging the active imagination enchanting and productive, both personally and professionally, I wanted to employ a very practical tool that could be easily adopted and was universally acceptable. My desire was to venture forth with it into the wider sphere of personal transformation. I don't remember how I arrived at the Intuitive Vision Board process while walking the dog because we never used them at university. However, I had been in the habit of making large collages with my daughter for some years prior to this. It was an activity we loved and shared and we always placed our masterpieces prominently to ponder them aloud. However, by the time the dog walk was over, I had crafted the entire creative process in my head and all that was needed was for me to set it down on paper.

Perhaps I was also influenced by an earlier life experience in which I had literally received a vision that caused me to faint (see Chapter 8 for this unusual account). Before then I had no interest in visions, vision quests or becoming a visionary. But from that moment on my curiosity was well and truly piqued. The question of how to replicate

01: Initiation

02: Invocation

03: Invention

04: Inception

05: Immersion

06: Illumination

07: Integration

08: Inauguration

the conditions that gave rise to this experience remained with me until my subsequent education in the creative process was grafted onto the front-end of my collaging hobby, and the Intuitive Vision Board was the manifest outcome. Finally, I was confident this intuitive tool would enable Remarkable-Right to speak up and allow more people to receive visionary guidance that could result in a personal transformation and the reinvention and redirection of their lives.

I've facilitated the Intuitive Vision Board workshop since 2008 to men, women and children – both as individuals and in organisations – with fascinating results as you can tell from their stories. By tacitly agreeing to give up the reins of control, they have allowed the genius to work through them.

If a person had been stuck in a rut or at their wits' end prior to making the Intuitive Vision Board, the process enabled them to turn around their situation and redefine it entirely, as was the case for Carl Jung. Meanwhile with images that were choosing them and with scissors and glue to hand, they set out to break new ground. After running a dozen or more workshops, it dawned on me that I'd not only structured the process to encourage emergent thinking but also, unintentionally, had replicated the conditions for receiving a vision in true visionary style like Moses. AHA!

In the next story let's look at what one visionary uncovered during the workshop itself and why it took her so long before she felt ready to come to me for subsequent coaching.

Breathing new life into a long-abandoned dream

"The beginning of a new year found me at the Intuitive Vision Board workshop. I was in my 40s and struggling with confusion around what to do with the next stage of my life. I'd had a good career yet I felt I wanted to find something more meaningful (not unusual after the age of 40, I guess).

"At the beginning of the session we were asked to spontaneously name an animal or creature and I remember my instantaneous response was a whirling dervish. That's me alright – my thoughts going around in circles, not finding a particular conclusion – was the way I looked at it. I later learnt that the spiral is a universal symbol of change and transformation.

01: Initiation

02: Invocation

03: Invention

04: Inception

05: Immersion

06: Illumination

07: Integration

08: Inauguration

"Making the Intuitive Vision Board itself was a real joy. It was such a luxury to spend time in my own world, choosing pictures and placing them on my board entirely judgement-free, analysis-free, blame-free, and in a limitless way. Because I wouldn't need to show this vision board to anyone, I could do whatever I liked. And I loved what I created."

It was eight months before I heard from Maureen. The reason for her pregnant pause can be summed up by the polar bear that appeared centre stage on her vision board and the word accompanying it: *adopting*. This had astounded her at the time and she needed time to process it. Adoption was something both she and her husband had seriously considered, then promptly forgotten about. Yet here it was, raising its head again years later. And because she'd created the vision board from her heart and not with her head, Maureen was smart enough to realise she was not to dismiss it a second time. Meanwhile, she saw herself as the polar bear – the big mama at the centre of the home and at the centre of family life, accompanied by several images of dogs. She had neither child nor dog at the time.

"At the end of the session when I stood back and looked at my vision board it all looked somewhat random and chaotic but it also pointed heavily towards adoption. Once I'd got over the initial shock, which took me about eight months to process, I booked a coaching session with Mary and talked through my board in depth. This gave me confidence and engendered a feeling of calm to progress in the direction of adoption. I believed in my heart this to be the right way, while the vision board was a point of reference I could return to when any of my old doubts tried to creep back in."

Maureen and her husband did pursue the lengthy adoption procedure with perseverance and determination. One year later they adopted a six-year-old boy and are thrilled to bits to have him. And to complete the rosy picture, they have added a puppy to the family who has proved to be more of a handful than their lovely son. All good wishes to this family whose happiness was enabled by Maureen's intuitive vision.

49

01: Initiation

02: Invocation

03: Invention

04: Inception

05: Immersion

06: Illumination

07: Integration

08: Inauguration

Seven ways to lure the genius out of the lamp

Over the years of working with people and their visions, here are seven conclusions I have reached on how to set the stage to become a visionary. Each activity alone encourages emergent thinking, as the accompanying endorsements from famous visionary predecessors demonstrate. It isn't necessary for each of these criteria to be present to receive a vision but, for good measure, I have incorporated them all into the Intuitive Vision Board process.

1. Change of environment

You must leave home behind to set sail on your odyssey, just like the Native Americans do on their vision quests and the Ancient Greeks on retreat in Chapter 2. A break with tradition is essential, otherwise you will be tempted to fall back into old patterns of behaviour and thinking, which are defined by the familiar space. When I work one-to-one with vision board clients I also like to include Feng Shui practice to ensure the environment in which they live and work in is in alignment with their unfolding vision, so the latter can come to fruition more easily. Consider how difficult it must be for a smoker to quit while living among a household of smokers.

Joan of Arc received her first vision while lounging in her father's garden, age 17. It was the first of many transmissions in which she gleaned enough insight to successfully lead an army against the English. Moses was alone on the mountain, quietly tending his sheep, when God appeared in the burning bush to bestow his mission. Eileen Caddy lived in simple accommodation, yet stole herself away each night to meditate in the toilet while the children were asleep. The guidance she received was the inspiration behind the building of Findhorn, the spiritual retreat centre in North East Scotland.

2. Stop doing, start being

The next requirement is to reduce – or eliminate – the continuous stream of thought that preoccupies Logical-Left brain. This is achieved quickest by slowing the pace, descending down through the gears, until you come to stillness in your mind, in silence. Disconnection from any kind of portable technology helps to get you into the right mindset and remain in the creative groove; your mind must be open, alert and empty,

01: Initiation

02: Invocation

03: Invention

04: Inception

05: Immersion

06: Illumination

07: Integration

08: Inauguration

not psyched-up and overstimulated. I favour a meditative practice in which you remain fully present in your body, such as a body-centred seated meditation, which we'll do together in the next chapter. Yoga, Pilates, and Tai Chi work too – or my favourite one of all is natural, improvised, mindful movement.

Mozart was gifted. He also recognised that a Remarkable-Right brain state of mind preceded all his creative breakthroughs. "When I am... completely myself, entirely alone and of good cheer – say travelling in a carriage or walking after a good meal, or during the night when I cannot sleep; it is on such occasions that my ideas flow best and most abundantly. Whence and how they come, I know not, nor can I force them... Nor do I hear in my imagination the parts successively, but I hear them... all at once. What a delight I cannot tell! All this inventing, this producing, takes place in a pleasing lively dream."

3. Enliven the senses

Sadly most of us have forsaken the notion of the sabbath where we took a whole day off each week without work or agenda. Imagine 24 hours without the computer, the phone or even the TV. Technology is so insistent and our senses are numbed by it, 24/7. Purposely taking a sabbatical gives you time to notice what is going on around you rather than constantly fishing for stimulation, information and entertainment. A meandering stroll through a forest. Walking barefoot along a beach. A wild swim in the sea. Climbing a tree. Any of these can reawaken your senses – sight, sound, touch, smell, taste – and help you become more receptive to the genius-in-waiting on the periphery of your conscious mind.

The composer Wagner, age 40, had a serious midlife crisis looming large. His music had run dry, his marriage was falling apart, his finances were in a shambles, and he was suffering badly from insomnia. He travelled for inspiration but found he tired easily. One day after a long country walk he flopped out on the couch. Half awake, half asleep, he heard a rushing noise form into the musical chord of E flat major. Sitting up in a state of shock he recognised the orchestral prelude to Das Rheingold. The inspiration he'd been waiting for was at last coming to him.

4. Try new things

To stimulate emergent thinking be willing to embark on a new project, learn a new skill and try on different experiences. Logical-Left will be inclined to talk you out of these adventures, with the excuse of an imminent deadline or time and money limitations. Override it. At a minimum, take a different route to the shops or for the school run and see what you notice. Better still, escape on your own for an hour for an *artist's date* (Julia

01: Initiation

02: Invocation

03: Invention

04: Inception

05: Immersion

06: Illumination

07: Integration

08: Inauguration

Cameron's invention in *The Artist's Way*). Visit a shop, a museum, a church or whatever calls for your attention. Take your time. Your aim is to disrupt your normal thought patterns and slip into experimental mode. You've seen how this worked for Carl Jung, although what he did made no logical sense to him while he was doing it. The chances are it can work for you.

5. Invite the muse

Allow for the unanticipated inspiration to arrive from an unexpected source; enter the muse. It's not very fashionable to speak in this way. However, Elizabeth Gilbert in *Big Magic* attests her worldwide success with writing *Eat Pray Love* as being propelled by a powerful, external force that felt wonderful to her while it was present. Both the Ancient Greeks and Romans were very familiar with the concept of the muse, believing as they did in the presence of *daimons* (note well the difference in spelling and connotation with the word "demon"). Working in cahoots with your daimon, it was felt, would bring you closest to your genius and allow you to attain the highest levels of happiness and fulfilment you were capable of. Eudaimonia is their word to describe this human flourishing, which loosely means *well-daimoned*.

Rudyard Kipling spoke openly about working with the muse: "Mine (daimon) came to me early when I sat bewildered among other notions. 'Take me and no other' it said. I obeyed and was rewarded. After that I learned to lean upon him and recognise the sign of his approach. If I ever held back anything... I paid for it by missing what I knew the tale lacked... When your daimon is in charge, do not try to think consciously. Drift, wait and obey."

6. Enter the dream-time

Once upon a time it was believed you could only enter the dream-time while asleep. Then Carl Jung showed us that to be asleep was unnecessary and you could enter the dream-time while remaining fully awake, using active imagination and the expressive arts process which we explored earlier in this chapter.

But for Elias Howe his genius spoke to him in a dream. For years he'd struggled to invent the lock stitch sewing machine and his early designs had a hole in the middle of the shank. Until the day came in which he had a nightmare and was commanded by the King, "upon the pain of death to finish it at once". As he was being led away by troops for execution, he glanced up and noticed their spears had eye-shaped holes near the top. He

01: Initiation

02: Invocation

03: Invention

04: Inception

05: Immersion

06: Illumination

07: Integration

08: Inauguration

spent the rest of the night awake, whittling away a new, improved needle with a hole at the top of the shank.

7. Be patient

There is a divine timing to events occurring and I've noticed that visions will not be rushed. It's out of your hands when your vision is to be born on the physical realm or parts thereof – and the pace at which it will unfold. During my visionary experience, which caused me to faint, which I talk about in Chapter 8, the full download came to me in one go and this certainly is the case when you create your Intuitive Vision Board. Yet it may be many weeks, months or years later that you understand what has been revealed to you. It is more likely the pieces of the puzzle will come together at different times and completing the jigsaw will not be possible in one go. In the interim, you must learn to trust it will happen; genius is at work here with infinite intelligence and you need to wait patiently in attendance until the dawning of clarity.

Now let's observe the genius at work on Laura's vision board.

The genius at work in decision-making

"I was at a bit of a crossroads when I bumped into Mary. I'd been in corporate life for 20+ years and enjoyed a good career in marketing and ended up in a very senior position, which involved an enormous amount of travelling. Ordinarily I would have loved this but it took me away from my family and I found this to be distressing. I was looking around for some other work to do.

"I came up with the idea for an online business that made housesitting and pet-sitting arrangements for homeowners across the world. The business was beginning to take off but we weren't quite in flow and there were some big decisions to be made. Mary suggested I make the Intuitive Vision Board to get some clarity. I'd never heard of it before and thought it was an odd idea but decided to give it a go."

53

01: Initiation

02: Invocation

03: Invention

04: Inception

05: Immersion

06: Illumination

07: Integration

08: Inauguration

Laura found making the Intuitive Vision Board to be enormously helpful in unlocking the decision-making that had her stuck and going around in circles. It enabled her to make some yes/no decisions quickly that were very influential in helping her move forward. She admitted it had seemed such a random exercise at the time – to be gathering images from magazines without any agenda. As she assembled her eclectic collection, she felt the process to be more like a dream with the images surfacing from the unconscious. It took her several months of waiting and talking it through with me, before it became apparent what the arrangement of images meant to her.

"The creative process had brought some of my real passions to the surface I'd lost touch with and reminded me to focus on these while moving the new business forward. My family were very central to the vision board and provided a clear motivation for me to make change. There were still lots of travel images on my board but, while it had been a burden in corporate life, I now realised the new business, which provided affordable travel options for house and petsitters to travel, could also do the same for us. Prompted by the Intuitive Vision Board, I'd turned my passion into a business, which didn't compromise my own desire for travel or exclude my family. The Intuitive Vision Board gave me the clarity I hadn't had before. I'm onto my third board now and I absolutely love making them for the surprises they reveal."

In the next chapter, Chapter 4 – Inception – I will talk you through how to prepare yourself to make the Intuitive Vision Board. Then in Chapter 5 – Immersion – I'll take you through the process itself, step by step.

Your intuitive vision is getting closer...

01: Initiation

02: Invocation

03: Invention

04: Inception

05: Immersion

06: Illumination

07: Integration

08: Inauguration

"All true artists, whether they know it or not, create from a place of no-mind, from inner stillness."

Eckhart Tolle, Spiritual Teacher

Chapter 4

INCEPTION

Preparation

By the time you've finished reading this book I hope you will have created your very own large and inspirational Intuitive Vision Board. It will hold all your most imaginative and visionary ideas together in one place, which you can refer back to at any time to remind yourself of the journey you are undertaking. I have never known anyone not be thrilled with their creation.

Making the Intuitive Vision Board is not an artistic process. Let me remind you it is instead the opportunity to give your creative intelligence a voice and bring to your notice important information that's hovering below the surface of your everyday attention. This *under-mind* can provide such a rich vein of ideas and guidance to encourage and support your well-being yet frequently its wisdom is overridden in favour of attending to the more pressing day-to-day matters.

In the previous chapter, we explored the different approaches to vision boarding and what thinking creatively means. Emergent thinking is what we are after and for it to predominate requires you to quieten Logical-Left, which we have seen will instinctively want to turn the vision board into a goal-setting exercise using pictures. This may be useful but it's not creative.

Instead, you will want to call on the Remarkable-Right to create a new, big picture, which may or may not build on anything you'd ever thought of before. The Intuitive Vision Board made in this way becomes a *gestalt* – a highly intelligent, organised field of information with specific properties that belong together. Its potency lies not in any single item grabbed hold of in isolation but in the sum of its component parts and their relationship to one another. It is a unified whole, which has a pattern to it; each image is important in and of itself and for its special contribution to the whole. These are the qualities of emergence for you.

57

01: Initiation

02: Invocation

03: Invention

04: Inception

05: Immersion

06: Illumination

07: Integration

08: Inauguration

Map of the creative terrain

To undertake the creative journey, therefore, requires you to consciously shift your attention from Logical-Left to Remarkable-Right in preparation. Here is a map of the territory to show you the difference between the two terrains.

EVERYDAY THINKING TERRAIN	INTUITIVE VISIONING TERRAIN
Left brain (LL) – logical, linear	Right brain (RR) – intuitive, non-linear
Beta waves – busy, quick, waking state	Alpha/Theta waves – slower, deeper, relaxed
Mind – conscious	Body-mind – unconscious, superconscious
Head – one centre of intelligence	Head, heart, gut – three centres of intelligence
Cognitive – 5–8% available intelligence	Under-mind – 92–95% available intelligence
Yang – masculine aspect of self	Yin – feminine aspect of self
Conditioned self	Authentic self
Wants	Needs
Active visualisation	Receptive visioning
Visual & auditory	Kinaesthetic
Verbal language – words	Poetic language – symbols, metaphors
Known – familiar, recognised	Unknown – surprises, mystery
Willpower to manifest	Magnetism to bring to fruition

From Beta to Alpha to Theta

As we track emergent visioning, it's worthwhile observing the correspondence between the different brain waves and the left and right hemispheres of the brain. When we relax to open and expand our minds, our brain waves shift from Beta to Alpha and eventually to Theta. Brain waves travel in spirals and the broader the spiral the more intuitive, more sensitive, more abstract your thinking capacity becomes.

Beta brain waves, which dominate our normal waking state of consciousness, are associated with Logical-Left. Our attention is directed towards cognitive tasks with security and stability top of the agenda. Beta moves fast as when we are engaged in problem-solving, decision-making or focused mental activity. And it dominates convergent thinking.

Continual high-frequency Beta processing is not an efficient way to run the brain since it takes a tremendous amount of energy. Many of us operate here so no wonder there is a high level of burnout and we find addictive ways of compensating to deal with this stress. Most makers of non-intuitive vision boards propagated on the internet would register Beta brain waves in the making. The vision board is yet another thing to be achieved to strike it off the to-do list.

Flowing Alpha is an idle, daydreaming state that begins to build a bridge between our inner and outer worlds such as when we are engaged in light meditation, pottering around or taking a walk. It is the resting state for the brain and serves to sustain mental coordination, calmness, mind/body integration, and learning. Alpha is the threshold to wisdom, intuition and creativity where ideas are distilled before being expressed. Alpha brain waves are both active and receptive in the way that divergent thinking engages both Logical-Left and Remarkable-Right.

In the Theta state you are much less able to focus on one thing at a time and so your language can appear vague and non-specific to others. Theta brain waves occur mostly in sleep but they also dominate deep meditation and the active dream-time, providing a gateway to the unconscious and superconscious realms. Theta brain waves are the most innovative and generative of all. In the final stages of making your Intuitive Vision Board you are tuned into the impulses originating from deep within.

For completeness, the slowest brain waves of all are Delta as when we are in dreamless sleep or the deepest meditation. These brain waves are essential to healing and regeneration and suspend time as we know it, often referred to as presence, oneness with the universe, and totality.

Towards the end of the Intuitive Vision Board workshop when everyone is in full flow, Beta brain waves have moved out, Alpha have moved in and the group will be touching on Theta. A stillness will have descended upon the room, which feels lighter and greatly expanded; it's a joy to experience.

Each type of brain wave clearly serves a function. In our busy-busy Logical-Left dominated world, we are most often banging the Beta drum, leaving little opportunity to drop into the others, which is perhaps why we have so few brain waves! We absolutely *do not* want to be in the Beta zone when creating the Intuitive Vision Board, which is why the next four preparatory exercises are so important and not to be skipped.

Body Full Meditation

If you dive straight into making your Intuitive Vision Board while Logical-Left is still active you now understand, from what's gone before, the outcome will be limited to what you know already. To give Logical-Left a break in my workshops we begin with a Body Full Meditation, which you can easily listen to at home. You may want to record the words that follow by speaking them slowly into your phone, with decent pauses in between each sentence. Or for an easy life, just listen to the recording on my website www.marynonde.com.

Sitting comfortably in a chair, where you won't be interrupted, allow yourself to rest back into it. You don't need to be overly concerned about having the perfect posture or your vertebrae stacked one on top of the other. Take this time to arrive and have a real sense of sitting there, allowing your weight to be borne by the chair, so you are not holding yourself up in any way. This may mean you are leaning backwards into the back rest of the chair, which is a good use for it, while your weight is descending with gravity through your sitting bones, into the chair itself.

Gradually allow your attention to drop down into your feet. If you are unable to feel the contact your feet have with the floor, take a good look at them and wriggle them around to remind yourself where they are. Perhaps even make a percussive sound with your feet before allowing them to finally come to rest on the floor. Then close your eyes.

01: Initiation

02: Invocation

03: Invention

04: Inception

05: Immersion

06: Illumination

07: Integration

08: Inauguration

01: Initiation

02: Invocation

03: Invention

04: Inception

05: Immersion

06: Illumination

07: Integration

08: Inauguration

With your attention now in the soles of your feet, allow these to soften and spread onto the floor. You may feel a warmth or tingling sensation as you do so. In your mind's eye allow yourself to visit each digit of the foot in turn. Don't worry if there are blanks in your awareness.

Now bring your attention to your instep and move upwards towards the ankle. Pause while you invite your ankle to soften and release so that more energy can flow down through your legs into your feet and out through the toes.

Travelling upwards from the ankle through the shin to the right-angle bend of the knee, pause while you invite your knee to soften and release. Continue travelling along the full length of the thigh, observing the contact it has with the seat of the chair. Finally you will arrive at the joint of your hips. Pause while you invite this juncture to soften and release.

Shift your attention into your sitting bones. Let your weight sink down once more through these as you observe again the contact your bottom has with the seat of the chair – at the same time you'll notice the sensation the soles of your feet have in contact with the ground.

Returning now to the base of your back, travel slowly upwards in your mind's eye through the vertical surface of your back, noticing the contact it has with the upright of the chair, until eventually you arrive at your shoulder line.

Pause while you invite your shoulder joints to soften and release to allow your arms to hang loosely from the shoulder sockets. Let the weight of your upper arm cascade down into your elbow joint. Pause as you invite your elbow to soften and release. Continue allowing your attention to flow down through your lower arms into your wrists. Pause as you allow your wrists to soften and release.

Finally, allow the energy to stream down through your hands and out through each fingertip in turn.

Observe where your hands are in contact with your body or the chair. Can you still feel where your back is resting against the upright of the chair, your bottom is resting on the seat of the chair with your weight descending through the sitting bones, and your feet are supported by the ground? Can you observe these four points of contact all at the same time? Don't worry if you can't. Just have the intention that you are able to do so.

Returning now to the base of your neck, travel upwards in your mind's eye to where your head is balanced on top of your spine. Make a slow tour of this sphere, starting on the left-hand side, moving around to the back of your head, then to the right-hand side, bringing your full attention to each surface in turn, inviting your features to soften and release as you do so, until finally you arrive at your face. Pause here a little longer to allow any tension in the face to soften and release, including your jaw muscles. Let your eyes rest back into their sockets.

Travel now to the crown of your head – the plane that is perpendicular to the ceiling. Invite this surface to soften, release, expand and open. Pause with your full awareness here – while also noticing the way your hands have settled onto your body or onto the chair, your back is leaning into the back rest of the chair, your bottom is supported by the seat, your feet are welcoming the contact with the floor. Rest here in stillness.

After a while allow your field of attention to expand to take in the sounds in the room itself. Without losing the sensation of your contact with the chair, allow your attention to expand even further to embrace the sounds outside the room too. Finally, allow your attention to expand as far as it possibly can to include the furthest sound you can hear, all the while not losing contact with your physical presence on the chair and the soles of your feet on the floor. Pause once more in stillness and spaciousness.

Now gently and leisurely rein your attention in, leaving behind the external sounds in the environment and slowly returning with full awareness into your body. Notice where your hands are resting in contact with your body or the chair. Notice where your back is supported by the back rest, your bottom supported by the seat of the chair, and the soles of your feet are in contact with the ground.

Gradually allow your eyes to open, keeping your gaze lowered, to allow the light to filter in through your peripheral vision first. When you are ready, let yourself move and stretch a little in a natural, unpremeditated way, all the while staying aware of the energy present in your body and the points of contact you have with the chair and the floor.

Take as much time as you need and only when you are ready come to standing. You are now ready for the next exercise.

01: Initiation

02: Invocation

03: Invention

04: Inception

05: Immersion

06: Illumination

07: Integration

08: Inauguration

Animal totem

As the participants in the workshop bring their attention back into the room, I ask them each to declare the first creature – animal, bird, aquatic, reptile or insect – that comes into their head, without thinking about it. Fictitious creatures like the phoenix are also allowed. I then ask for the first colour that springs to mind and a word or two to describe what the creature is doing.

Try this for yourself now. With your feet firmly planted on the floor and your full awareness in your body, say out loud the first animal that comes to mind, the first colour, and what it is doing too. Don't become heady about the task and concerned about whether you are giving the right answer – or what it might mean. Be playful with it. Let the words pop out of your mouth. When you are in a light and carefree frame of mind, you are most connected to Remarkable-Right and potentially at your most creative.

This is the first of three exercises in improvisation that can be very insightful, rather like picking a tarot card spontaneously from a pack and exploring its implications. In this instance, the creature describes a more animalistic and primitive energy that resonates with you at a deep level rather like the shaman's power animal. By investigating the creature's qualities you can draw upon them to assist you in manifesting your vision.

There are many interpretations of the symbolic value of creatures available on the internet. The top 12 creatures cited in my workshop are listed below along with their associated symbolism derived from *Animal Speak* by Ted Andrews. He references animals, birds, insects and reptiles in alphabetical order throughout his book:

>> **Dolphin.** The healing power of the breath, sound, and water.
>> **Elephant.** Ancient power, wisdom and strength. Primordial royalty.
>> **Tiger.** Passion, power, devotion and sensuality. New adventures.
>> **Lion.** Creativity, intuition, imagination. Feminine energy.
>> **Eagle.** Spirit and growth. Alchemy and power.
>> **Dog.** Faithfulness, protection, companionship.
>> **Cat.** Mystery, magic, independence, curiosity.
>> **Bear.** The power of the unconscious. Inner resources. Nurturing.
>> **Panther.** Reclaiming true power, ferocity, valour.
>> **Owl.** Magic, omens, silent wisdom, visionary.
>> **Butterfly.** Transformation, transmutation, colourful, joy.
>> **Otter.** Playful, nurturing, joy, sharing.

The colour you have chosen to associate with the creature will describe something about the energy you require or the mood you will need to be in to cultivate your vision. It does not have to be the literal colour: a purple horse or a green pig is quite acceptable. Every colour in the visible light spectrum has its own wavelength and vibrates at a different frequency, which produces a specific energy and has a different nourishing effect. There are many descriptions of what the colours mean on the internet and their associations with the chakras (the energy centres in the body). If you are interested in learning more, I also provide a summary in Chapter 6.

The action or descriptive word(s) you have ascribed to your creature, such as what it's doing and the speed or manner in which it is moving, conveys something you could do with more of in your life. You may be surprised to find your creature is skipping, which might suggest you could be more energetic or need to lighten up. Or when a normally terrestrial bear is flying through the tree tops, it could imply your intuitive abilities, typically associated with the bear, are going to develop rapidly to propel you forward. Because so many of us survive on adrenalin with too much nervous energy coursing through us, I find plenty of sleeping creatures curled up in a ball in a protective hollow attend the Intuitive Vision Board workshop.

How the totem animal who appeared in this preparatory exercise can work its presence onto the Intuitive Vision Board itself is the subject of the next story.

Totem animal stars on the Intuitive Vision Board

Gaynor describes her totem encounter:

"When I was in my early teens, I announced I would one day live in Vancouver. I had no idea where the notion came from. Now in my 50s, I had still never been there although I have friends in Canada and just across the border in the US.

"In my latest Intuitive Vision Board I had a picture of waterside Vancouver. I was delighted to see this because meanwhile I'd completely forgotten about my desire to go there. Soon after the workshop, out of the blue, I was invited to Vancouver to participate in a training event being run by a friend and colleague who I'd worked with years ago. I snapped it up.

01: Initiation

02: Invocation

03: Invention

04: Inception

05: Immersion

06: Illumination

07: Integration

08: Inauguration

"Getting to Vancouver was the fulfilment of the long-held but half-forgotten dream and I absolutely fell in love with it. Just wandering around the city soaking it up was a hugely enriching experience for me – a few days of pure exploration and freedom from work, enjoying the closeness of the sea and the mountains alongside, with the proximity of the urban buzz and all the city has to offer. In six days I just scratched the surface and was already planning a return visit.

"Here's another funny thing. The animal that sprang to my mind in the workshop was a turquoise otter who I described as 'curious'. I've always loved otters but never considered I had a particular affinity with them so I was surprised it came up this time. Much to my delight, sea otters showed up with some abundance and in various guises while I was in Vancouver – in art, during random chats, both in the aquarium and in the wild. I was quite mystified by them but took this as confirmation that I was in the right place at the right time."

In a coaching session later with Gaynor we explored the key notes associated with the otter: joyful, playful, nurturing and sharing. They are also naturally curious and frisky. Their connection with water (sea or river) links them to the primal aspects of our feminine nature – creation, imagination, and love of the young. I felt that Gaynor was being reminded to keep her inner child alive and well, alongside her commitment to her career, and not to sacrifice one for the other. The otter can also indicate the desire to have a real child as this next story illustrates.

I too visited similar coastal waters to Gaynor having ventured to Seattle for my training in Feng Shui. Beforehand I took a trip out to visit the magnificent San Juan Islands off the coast of British Columbia. Walking along a deserted driftwood beach I approached a rocky headland when suddenly a large group of sea otters, called a romp, emerged from behind the rocks – about 30 of them. I was stunned and froze in my tracks as I watched them play on the rocks then make their way into the sea. Two remained "romping" in front of me about four metres away. They were in no hurry. Casually playing together, always in physical contact with one another, before slipping into the sea.

That night back in my bed & breakfast I randomly decided I was ready to have a child. Within six months I was pregnant. I wasn't in the habit of making the Intuitive Vision Board back then but I was in the habit of paying attention to the signs from the natural kingdom.

Trust Walk – partner

Now you are present in your body after the Body Full Meditation and you are in a playful mode with your animal totem alongside, it's time to come to your feet – and to your senses. Take a moment to register how much awareness you have retained in your body and whether it has drifted back up into your head. If so, consciously send it down into the soles of your feet.

This exercise should be conducted with the partner who is sharing the Intuitive Vision Board process with you. If you are doing it on your own, there is an alternative version later but I recommend you read this whole section first to understand the purpose of the process.

The Trust Walk is both intriguing and calming. Its purpose is to help you register how fully present you are in your whole body and therefore present to life. If you feel nervous doing it that's actually an important piece of information for you.

Even if you've done it many times before, the experience is always different as you discover how you are responding to life in this moment. It's preferably an outdoor exercise that isn't weather dependent if you are prepared to dress for it. I once led a Trust Walk in the rain with everyone togged up appropriately in waterproof jackets and with colourful umbrellas. The rain added an extra dimension to the exercise. However, if venturing outside proves too impractical the Trust Walk can equally well take place indoors. It works in the same way – to awaken the senses throughout the whole body – but the overall experience is different, neither better nor worse. My personal preference, however, is for the outdoors.

In my workshop people buddy up and each pair has an eye mask between them. You can do this exercise without an eye mask although the temptation to cheat by peeping is great. Taking it in turns, one is the leader and the other the follower; it is the latter who wears the eye mask first. You are taking a Trust Walk together and the leader has the eyes for both of you.

Start by giving your follower plenty of time to become orientated and at ease with the eye mask on by standing still first. Remind your follower to bring their attention down into their feet and to feel them fully on the ground, as we did in the Body Full Meditation. This way their senses can begin to awaken to their 360 degree surroundings. Using your non-dominant hand, gently cup their elbow to allow the weight of their arm to yield to

01: Initiation

02: Invocation

03: Invention

04: Inception

05: Immersion

06: Illumination

07: Integration

08: Inauguration

01: Initiation

02: Invocation

03: Invention

04: Inception

05: Immersion

06: Illumination

07: Integration

08: Inauguration

your hand. Then gently take their wrist with your dominant hand so their arm doesn't flop around. You are now ready to take them on a guided walk in silence.

There is a tendency perhaps from embarrassment, shyness, or fear of getting it wrong, to want to talk throughout this exercise. But it is so much more powerful if you resist the tendency and conduct it in silence. A good leader will assume their leadership confidently but not by gripping hold of their follower for dear life because you'll inject your tension into their body. You must train yourself to become sensitive to your follower and read the signs as to their comfort or discomfort through the contact you have with them. This requires you to be fully present in your whole body too and not just in your head. It also requires you to walk at a pace which allows your follower to become increasingly at ease while walking blindfolded. Start slowly then build up the pace.

Don't underestimate how challenging this is when so many of us are culturally conditioned to be visually dominant. The whole purpose of this exercise is for both the leader and the follower to retain their attention throughout their whole body while awakening their other senses – hearing, smell, touch (including temperature), kinaesthetic movement, taste. The latter is limited perhaps unless you are indoors and have prepared some food beforehand, which you can lead your follower to sample.

Take your follower on a good long walk and make sure you do not lead them around in a circle in one direction only; vary the lead. Once you feel your follower is more at ease, the next development is to guide them to a variety of stimuli and allow them to reach out and discover what's there through touch. Don't rush this – allow plenty of time for them to enjoy a full encounter.

As the leader, you need to check in regularly with yourself that you are still present in your own body while also experiencing your partner's Trust Walk vicariously, rather than allowing your attention to drift. Only when the follower has finished their current exploration is it time to decide where you are going to take them next rather than anticipating your next move in advance.

After ten minutes or so, the leader brings their follower to a standstill by resting their hands on their shoulders to signify the Trust Walk is over. Gently withdraw your hands and stand back from your follower, leaving them with the eye mask on. Invite them to take their time integrating the experience and to register how their body is feeling. Only then will the follower remove their eye mask and you will be ready to swop over.

Resist the temptation to talk at this stage. Wait until you have both had a turn before exchanging your experiences and observations. There's always a lot to share with each

01: Initiation

02: Invocation

03: Invention

04: Inception

05: Immersion

06: Illumination

07: Integration

08: Inauguration

other and a lot to learn about yourself. It's worth taking a moment to write this down because you won't remember it later on.

Trust Walk – solo

If you are creating an Intuitive Vision Board on your own, I invite you to be bold and have a tiny experience of what life might be like as a blind person. In advance, prepare a worktop or dining room table – either inside or outside the house – with a variety of objects of all shapes, sizes and textures, which you can lift and handle. I would also include some foods and drink you can sample too.

But before you get stuck into this medley, I invite you to venture out into the garden, accompanied by a long-handled umbrella, a bamboo cane or a walking stick. You are going to use this to sense what is in front of you once your eye mask is in position. If you're feeling bold, you can do this without a stick – but move very slowly with both hands extended in front of you and with no tension creeping into the arms. Allow your attention to drop down into your feet so you become very aware of the ground supporting you. With your stick gently tapping in front of you, start to edge forward. When you encounter an obstacle, move towards it slowly with your arms outstretched, your stick tucked away underneath your arm. Give yourself time to enjoy the encounter through touch before moving on. The same exercise can be conducted inside the house.

The Trust Walk is a wonderful exercise and brings you back into the now like nothing else, even better than sitting still in meditation. It demands your full attention to remain alert and to prevent yourself from falling over. It correspondingly awakens all three centres of intelligence in the body: gut/belly (instincts), heart (feelings) and head (thinking). There is a tendency to live in your head, which this exquisite quote from James Joyce describes beautifully in his book *The Dubliners*. "Mr Duffy lived a short distance from his body." Isn't it true? However, when you are fully awake, integrating and acting on information received by all three centres, then you are duly able to respond to life more fully and more intelligently. Three receiving stations working in unison leads to an enormous increase in our strength, power and wisdom. It helps you lead a more balanced life, which will enhance your relationships and allow you to engage more mindfully with the world around you. When you live out of your head alone, you will never arrive anywhere in one piece as the next story illustrates.

Among the olive groves

I was attending a week-long dance-movement workshop in an ancient olive grove in Italy with 20 other dancers. In theory we were all regularly connected to our bodies through our practice. We were set a task in pairs. One of us had to go to the top of a gently inclined slope while our partner waited for us at its base about 20 metres away. The one at the top was given instructions to roll down the slope, like you might have done as a child, to your partner at the bottom – but this time slowly and with full awareness of rolling. This may sound like a simple and crazy exercise. But it isn't. It's quite profound and the results were most illuminating.

Only three out of the ten pairs finished up together at the bottom. Because I'd rolled down the slope very quickly, not what was required, it meant nevertheless that I had time to look around and watch what else was occurring. Most people had begun to roll off course very early on but hadn't noticed and just kept going. The further down the inclination they got, the further adrift they became until they were a long way removed from their partner at the bottom. If they had been present in their whole body (all three centres of intelligence awake and working together) and not just in their heads, they would have recognised what was happening and rectified their course.

However, the three centres of intelligence within were in a world of their own. Their head thinking: I wonder what the point of all this is. Their heart feeling: this is lovely but it would be much better on the softer grass than on hard, dry ground. The gut saying: let's just get to the bottom and then we can all go to lunch. All three centres had contrary agendas, pulling in three different directions, and nobody taking overall control of these impulses. The result? Unpredictable, chaotic, and certainly no chance of reaching the partner at the bottom of the slope. This is a very fine metaphor for what can happen in life when we are blissfully unaware of how our energy is pulling us in three different directions simultaneously.

01: Initiation

02: Invocation

03: Invention

04: Inception

05: Immersion

06: Illumination

07: Integration

08: Inauguration

Creative installation

This is the final exercise to prepare you for making the Intuitive Vision Board. This one encourages you to be experimental, to play and to commit yourself to taking action without anticipating whether you are doing it right or wrong. It also encourages you not to adopt a fixed position too quickly. Once again I will describe the exercise as if you were undertaking it with a creative companion. Equally well, you can carry it out on your own, which then bears resemblance to the sand tray therapy used by psychotherapists, particularly when working with children.

You are about to create an installation, which can be dismantled easily at the end of the session. Each person needs to arrive with a minimum of six everyday objects (from the home or the garage) – anything that catches your eye for no apparent reason other than it pleases you. If you are playing on your own, gather together three times as many.

These objects are going to be moved around quite vigorously to make a creative installation and there are to be no limitations placed on how the objects can be used. I suggest therefore you avoid using anything too precious or sacred in case it gets damaged. Participants should in any case be briefed to take care when handling the objects. If you feel uncomfortable about seeing your precious Buddha stood on its head, which can happen as the party gets underway, it's best to leave it out of the equation. The creation is dismantled at the end of the workshop so nothing will be left behind.

If you are working with a companion your six objects will consist of: two large-scale objects e.g. the size of a guitar or lamp; two medium-scale objects e.g. a scarf or a cushion; two small-scale objects e.g. an egg or an ornament. On your own, you'll need six of each size object. Gather these all together to one side, close to where you plan to make the installation. You are going to assemble these items onto a table or the floor so you need to be able to retrieve them easily from where they are stored. You must be able to approach the surface you're working on without obstruction. You also need to leave space all around the installation to be able to manoeuvre yourself and the objects freely, while also being able to view the emerging installation from all sides.

Each person selects an object randomly from the collection and places it in the installation. The purpose of the exercise is to allow the creative impulse to arise in you without thinking too hard about it in advance, and then committing yourself to acting on this impulse. Objects once positioned can be moved around freely, by acting on a whim, without anyone deciding why that is. You'll also get used to seeing what you placed in

01: Initiation

02: Invocation

03: Invention

04: Inception

05: Immersion

06: Illumination

07: Integration

08: Inauguration

the installation, moved or removed by another, and noticing any feelings that arise as a consequence. The exercise is conducted in silence; nobody tells anybody what to do or how to do it. The instructions are given at the start to keep the process clean. They are:

- » No talking
- » Stay present in your whole body as you select one object at a time
- » Don't decide in advance what object to choose
- » You can select any object – yours or another's
- » Place the object in the installation without anticipating where it's going
- » Anyone can move the objects – or remove them from the scene entirely – at any time
- » Just a few people place objects at a time so it doesn't become chaotic
- » Keep moving. Don't stand still on the sidelines because your attention will drift off
- » Circulate around the installation constantly to refresh your perspective
- » View the installation from different levels besides standing: bend down, lie down
- » Keep going until there is an unspoken consensus that the installation is complete

You will be astounded by what is created without verbal instruction or anyone managing the process. There are other developments to this exercise which I include in my workshop but the next step is very significant. Now you get to place yourself in the installation. Where do you feel drawn to be? Depending on the room available, you can either literally position yourself there, not analysing why that is. Or, if this is not practical without destroying the installation, locate yourself as close to where you'd like to be, which still gives you the perspective of the whole that most appeals to you.

Once everyone has taken up a position, ask each other to describe what they see, feel and imagine from their perspective and what it is that has drawn them to that particular spot. You may find yourself at first describing what you literally see. However, the intention is to quickly move on by associating what you see with something you imagine is happening from your perspective. Also take note of where you are and how you are fixed in relation to others. In this exercise you are using your active imagination I first raised in Chapter 3 so allow yourself to experiment, improvise – and don't hold back. You can't get it wrong.

By now, you will have learned something more about your real wants, desires and aspirations that are lurking below your day-to-day reality and have surfaced through these embodiment exercises. It's worth making a note of your experiences before you move on to Chapter 5 – Immersion – which is how to make the Intuitive Vision Board itself.

01: Initiation

02: Invocation

03: Invention

04: Inception

05: Immersion

06: Illumination

07: Integration

08: Inauguration

"You must give birth to your images. They are the future, waiting to be born. Fear not the strangeness you feel. The future must enter into you long before it happens..."

Rainer Maria Rilke, Poet

Chapter 5

IMMERSION

What I enjoy most about the Intuitive Vision Board process is that it's do-able and achievable by just about anybody. My youngest creator to date was a four-year-old, who accompanied her mother to the workshop. She insisted on making her own vision board and did a wonderful job of wielding the scissors unaided. My oldest creator to date was a spiritual leader in her late 70s, whose attention at that stage in her life was purely transpersonal and concerned with what she might leave behind as a legacy. I've also worked with people who are very sick in hospital or confined to the home. They were able to choose the images for themselves but unable to cut them out and stick them down. However, with my help, they could still create an empowering vision board to give them a new horizon to contemplate beyond their current malaise.

Before I take you step by step through the process of creating your own Intuitive Vision Board let me share a story about finding love to inspire you along the way. Rowena has made several vision boards with me and here she is describing what happened for her with the first two.

On finding love

"I live in a lovely village in Cannock Chase, an area of outstanding natural beauty midway between Manchester and Birmingham. There are fields at the back of my house and just enough shops, plus a café within walking distance, to feel like I belong to a community. I am married to a gorgeous man and we're both self-employed.

"When I made my first Intuitive Vision Board it was a different story. I was stuck in a long-term relationship that wasn't going well but I didn't have the courage to leave it. To my surprise there was a photo on my board of a woman standing alone with her back to the camera. I remember thinking: this is a clear confirmation; it is time for you to go Rowena. Seeing this appear so vividly gave me the confidence to see it through – and after the workshop I ended the relationship. This action alone released a massive amount of pent-up energy in me and with it came real clarity. I knew what I needed to do on every level and I was swept along by waves of synchronicity; everything fell into place and every day something magical happened.

01: Initiation

02: Invocation

03: Invention

04: Inception

05: Immersion

06: Illumination

07: Integration

08: Inauguration

"During this time of transition I made a second vision board with Mary. Three things about it stood out for me. A pair of shoes – and for some curious reason I was drawn to buy a similar pair soon after the workshop. Mary told me that shoes can symbolise standing on new foundations and moving forward, which I thought was very appropriate. Images of English countryside appeared all over my board, very similar to where I am living now and where my husband and I do a lot of walking. And finally there were two redheaded children running around…!

"Perhaps I became a bit overwhelmed by the influx of new energy coursing through me or perhaps I just needed to slow it down but I fell ill. In spite of this, a normally unassuming friend pressurised me into attending a chanting session with her. It was a powerful evening and I came home with a clear head. Back home I sat down to write about it and a dating site profile fell out onto the paper unprompted. I stuck it up next to my vision board and that night received a text from my first suitor.

"Among the various men who showed up, one stood out. He was so seductive and forthcoming he took my breath away. We exchanged emails frequently and spoke on the phone often but because he lived in Manchester and I in Oxford, we'd not yet met. Then I received an invitation to an event he'd organised in Glasgow. I hesitated only momentarily before jumping on a plane to join him and we spent our first date celebrating with his team mates. By the third date he declared he loved me. By the fourth date, he asked me about having the children I'd mentioned on my Guardian Soulmates profile.

"A few weeks later we headed off to Sri Lanka and made our life plan together. My husband jokes that I imagined him into existence by making the vision board and writing the profile, because we are so well-suited. I couldn't have wished for a more thoughtful, respectful, kind and gorgeous man. And to complete the picture, we already have one gorgeous redheaded child…"

To complete Rowena's story I called her in the process of writing this book to advise her that the book was going to print with her account in it. I didn't hear back immediately but two days later I spotted a post on Facebook to advise her community she'd had a baby – the second of the two redheaded children on her vision board had now manifested. How special is that! I did hear from her eventually to say that she'd completely forgotten about the second redheaded child on her vision board in the interim.

Ready, steady, go... Now it's time for you to tune into your intuitive vision and see what magic you can weave by making your very own Intuitive Vision Board. Here are the materials you'll need to gather together in advance.

Mount board

I recommend using the largest size mount board available: A1. I like mount board because it stands up on its own without you having to frame your Intuitive Vision Board to hang it – and you'll want to display it prominently once it's complete. In my workshops I offer the choice between black or white mount board to work on. If you go into an art shop to buy your board you may be tempted by the range of colours available. However, I recommend you stick with a neutral colour otherwise the colour you choose may prejudice your vision with a particular vibrational energy in advance and you want to allow the images to determine the colour and the energetic tone of your board.

Timings

It's best to give yourself plenty of time so don't expect to have your Intuitive Vision Board complete within the hour. If you do so, it is more likely that Logical-Left is behind it and has already determined how much time this activity should take and how it can be squeezed into your busy schedule. This interference kills creativity. My workshop is four hours long for a good reason; half the time is spent getting into the right mindset, which we explored at length in Chapter 4. Therefore working on your own or with a buddy, the minimum time I would allow for the process is three hours.

Assuming you've prepared the space in which you're going to work in advance and assembled all the pieces you need beforehand then carve up the time as follows: one hour to warm up and get into the zone; a comfortable hour for flicking through magazines; a half hour to select and arrange the images; a half hour to stick them down. And you'll want to allow extra time at the end to look at each other's boards and to exchange the highlights with one another, if you've been sharing the creative space with a buddy. Otherwise, you will certainly want to share your board with your partner, friend or your children as soon as you can.

Environment

Before you start the Intuitive Vision Board process – even before you do the Body Full Meditation, the Trust Walk and the Creative Installation – you need to prepare the

01: Initiation
02: Invocation
03: Invention
04: Inception
05: Immersion
06: Illumination
07: Integration
08: Inauguration

75

01: Initiation

02: Invocation

03: Invention

04: Inception

05: Immersion

06: Illumination

07: Integration

08: Inauguration

environment you will be making the board in. Ideally find yourself a spacious room which is sufficiently warm, has lots of natural daylight and overlooks the garden or is in close proximity to nature.

You don't want to be interrupted so switch off your mobile: no beeping or vibrating. Unplug the landline if necessary; it is distracting to hear it ring and then click to engage the answerphone, let alone to hear the message being left. Be prepared to ignore the doorbell; switch it off too if you can. And no TV or radio playing in the background. Light ambient or meditative music is suitable while you are making the vision board. However, avoid songs or music with an insistent beat, both of which can influence your creativity when you want the inspiration to arise from within. I prefer not to play any music at all but to allow the natural sounds of the environment to fill the space.

Have water to drink and glasses close by. The obvious time for a comfort break is just after the preparatory exercises and before you embark on making your vision board. I recommend you keep the break short so you stay in the creative zone, which you've prepared well for. Avoid chatting since that too will engage Logical-Left, steal your time, and take you off course.

Work surface

I give people the choice as to whether they'd like to work on the floor or on the table. I'd have both options available when creating on your own or with a buddy. Making the Intuitive Vision Board is not a messy business and so long as you have a rubbish bin to hand to collect the snippets of paper, you don't need to be overly concerned. I once held a private workshop in a luxurious home with many expensive carpets and objets d'art around us. Eight of us managed perfectly well without having to make an insurance claim.

Glue, scissors and magazines

Once you have gathered up a pile of magazines (allow eight per person), scissors and glue you are ready to begin. I like glue sticks because they are easy to handle, solvent free and any splodges wash off easily. I also suggest you have two different size glue sticks because the smaller size is less inclined to tear the smaller images than a big stick would.

Since it goes against everything I stand for when it comes to creative improvisation, I recommend with a passion you don't arrive to make your board with a pile of images you have cut out earlier. I sincerely believe that every image you'll ever need for this creative meditation will be there among the random selection of magazines you have assembled.

01: Initiation

02: Invocation

03: Invention

04: Inception

05: Immersion

06: Illumination

07: Integration

08: Inauguration

If you don't find what you are looking for it's because you are not supposed to be looking for something specific in the first place. That's why I also discourage you from sourcing images using an online tool like Pinterest and steer you away from photo libraries. When you visit them you will already have a preconceived idea of what you want and will be searching under a particular topic, which leaves your intuition twiddling its thumbs and defeats the object of the Intuitive Vision Board.

In my workshops, I offer a wide variety of magazines with lots of pictures: fashion, lifestyle, weekend colour supplements, plus *National Geographic* and photographic magazines for quality imagery. I also suggest people bring one magazine that covers a hobby or interest area they like plus a magazine they wouldn't normally buy but for some reason catches their eye. I recommend you approach it in a similar way when assembling magazines at home.

Words v images

Avoid words, phrases or sentences, particularly if you are habitually a wordy person. Certainly don't go snapping up words before you have already assembled a whole pile of images. Words are inclined to the left brain and their potential is limited in meaning by their definition. Unless they are poetic in nature, words can quickly dominate a board and your attention gravitates towards them first. Images fare better; a picture speaks a thousand words is a useful idiom to remember when it comes to intuitive visioning. The complexity of an idea can best be conveyed with an image or images than a written description.

In the following story, we can see how the Intuitive Vision Board predicts new beginnings and how images are far more evocative than words in doing so.

The quest for individuation

I heard from a client, Leonie, who was going through a separation and asked if there were any indications on the vision board she'd made two months earlier. Leonie commented on the number of strong, feminine, independent images on her board and the repeating circular motifs. For example, prominent in the centre stood a woman contained yet splayed within a large hoop, her arms outstretched as if she was using all her strength to push the hoop apart. The circle is a universal symbol for wholeness so it was evident to me that Leonie might be ready to explore the edges of who she is really and was on a quest for individuation.

There was an image of a baby boy on her board too, although Leonie said she'd only just removed it. "You see, I was pregnant with a boy at the time of making the vision board and I'm not anymore. And as I removed the baby, another picture came away with it – that of a man and woman looking as if they'd just got married. How fascinating, I thought to myself, especially since it was my decision to end the relationship I was in because I felt I'd never truly be able to shine or feel like an empowered woman if I continued in it."

In removing both these images Leonie found they'd been concealing some striking imagery underneath: the ochre-red fissures of the Grand Canyon and another of a shoal of fish circling in the deep blue sea alongside. Red is traditionally the colour for energy/action/passion and blue indicates calm/depth/penetration. Consequently there was already a great deal of transformational energy expressed on Leonie's vision board, both in the colours and the content of the images she'd chosen. She went on to say:

"It's so curious because now I am consciously aware of the huge personal transformation taking place in me but I was not aware of this when I made the vision board nor had I begun the journey through it. For example, I've put myself forward for work I'd never have had the confidence to go after before. I feel like one of the many butterflies on my board that's just emerged from its cocoon – and there's no going back."

Leonie had another interesting insight. Just before her relationship ended, she fell in love with a piece of original art work. She described this as having *a fire in her belly for it* although it cost more than anything she'd ever spent on art before. After she got it home, she discovered it was almost identical to an image already on her vision board. She felt the purchase meant more to her than the painting itself, which she loved anyway. It represented her need to take an independent decision and act on it rather than being controlled by her ex all the time. Two days later she found the energy and determination to end the relationship – such was the transformational quality of the painting and colours. She kept the picture wrapped up until her ex had left the family home. When she was in a position to display it, she said she wept tears of freedom and joy.

01: Initiation

02: Invocation

03: Invention

04: Inception

05: Immersion

06: Illumination

07: Integration

08: Inauguration

Now the floor is yours. Here is my nine-step guide to making the Intuitive Vision Board from start to finish. Enjoy the process and savour every moment. I suggest you allocate at least three hours for the delightful self-indulgence of flicking through magazines, selecting images, and sticking them down.

1. Leaf

Always give yourself plenty of time to leaf through the magazines. This is such a luxury when you have no specific agenda in mind. Allow the images to come to you rather than hunting for them. Tear out anything that catches your eye without needing to know why. It could be the colour, the shape, the texture, the image itself, plus the odd word or short phrase. Don't try and guess what any of it might mean or why you have chosen them. Besides, the interpretation you give it today might take on an entirely different connotation three months on. This is very common and it's all part of the magic of intuitive visioning.

You are advised to tear out the whole page which contains the image, even if there is only one section you are planning to use. This maintains the momentum of leafing and avoids the tendency for Logical-Left to want to step in and focus on one image in particular and draft a whole story around what it might mean for you.

Some makers are completely mystified by almost all of the images appearing on their board. How exciting is that! Months later, as the pennies drop, they will have discovered a whole lot more about what they truly needed as opposed to what they thought they wanted. You may be convinced you know already what will appear on your vision board. But I wager this is your ego second-guessing for you and this is no guarantee it's in alignment with your deeper self. In the meantime, relax into the process and allow yourself to be delighted and bemused by whatever calls for your attention.

2. Sift and sort

After all that leafing you will have amassed a pile of pages to sift through for the images – or parts of images – that you are actually going to use. Remember, you're not looking for anything to represent your career, your romantic life or any already-known aspiration. So quell the Logical-Left and allow your Remarkable-Right to single out the images intuitively that will actually make it onto your board. Trust the process; you'll know what belongs on there without knowing why.

Don't worry if you still have an attachment to some images you eventually decide to discard. By the end of the creative process you will either have moved on from them entirely or held onto them for another purpose. I've also known a few people have so many images that they make a second vision board on the reverse of the first, with each side having quite a different quality to it. In extreme cases people take a second board and cover both sides like wallpaper in the same time it has taken others to complete one side.

3. Cut or tear

In the spirit of slow and tactile, I'll leave it open to you whether you want to cut around the image or tear around it for a different effect. Or a mixture of both. Some people like to square off their images and others to cut a shape to suit the picture. Both are right. And your style can change from one vision board to the next so be prepared for this. Your method today is not a fixed feature of your vision boarding style but is conveying something particular you are wanting to express in this moment.

By now you should feel very confident and impassioned about what is morphing onto your Intuitive Vision Board and how it is coming together. So don't be alarmed if you find yourself chopping off sections of a picture or reassembling parts of others to create different combinations; a human head appearing on an animal body for example, or replacing a face with another. It's all part of you claiming ownership of your intuitive vision.

4. Arrange

You are now ready to arrange the images on your board. With the same open attention and spirit of experimentation with which you made the creative installation earlier, you are going to proceed now. You will find that one image at a time will call you and want to belong in a certain section of your board. As more images crowd into the picture, you will find yourself shifting them around, taking them off, putting them back on again and never once stopping to dwell over why. You became accustomed to working in this way through making the creative installation.

In time, the images will find their favourite spot and certain pictures will decidedly belong together. Some will want to overlap and others will want to stand alone with space all around them. Yours is not to guess the reason why. Keep following your instincts.

Mostly, makers stay within the perimeter of their vision board but it's not uncommon to have photos hanging off the side – again this can change from one creative sitting to the next. Eventually, when you step back from your finished board, you will have created a

01: Initiation

02: Invocation

03: Invention

04: Inception

05: Immersion

06: Illumination

07: Integration

08: Inauguration

01: Initiation

02: Invocation

03: Invention

04: Inception

05: Immersion

06: Illumination

07: Integration

08: Inauguration

visionary road map. A veritable lifescape. It will start to work on you immediately from the inside, guiding you in certain directions and goading you into situations, all of which are necessary for your vision to unfold.

5. Stick

The next step is to commit the images to your board. At this stage, the Intuitive Vision Board workshop is in full swing and the same will be true for you at home. Not that you will be able to observe this yourself but I know from experience that an invisible transcendence will have infiltrated the room, which now feels alive with possibility. In the workshop, everyone is totally engaged in the task and no-one has the time for idle chatter or looking across to compare their work with a neighbour's. I am expecting by now that you too will be well and truly in the zone.

Taking the time to stick is important because you want the board to hold together for at least a year. Images can get damaged and curl up when their edges overlap the board or if they're not stuck down properly. It's worth checking too that everything is glued before you stand the board upright to gaze at your masterpiece. I once lifted a woman's completed vision board to place it in the workshop gallery as the rest of the group had finished and were waiting to do a tour. I was mortified to discover that not a single image had been stuck down; she groaned gracefully and then got back to arranging once more.

6. Share

A showcase of Intuitive Vision Boards is really quite a spectacle to behold. The finale to my workshop therefore is the parade of vision boards. Everyone has the chance to say a few words about some key images and what intrigues them most in the moment, knowing this might change over time. Not only is the diversity of vision boards fascinating but also when people are sharing their brief stories, it can often trigger suggestions and memories among listeners as aspects of their own boards or their own lives surface that they had not previously considered. Invariably people find themselves drawn to some boards more than others, besides their own. Conversations are struck up and relationships form which supersede the workshop.

You will want to share with your vision board buddy if you have one. Remember this is not about finding a Logical-Left explanation for everything or post-justification of why you have chosen certain images. If you are working alone, you will not have this opportunity until your partner or your offspring return home.

Alternatively, you could invite a friend over because it's very worthwhile to recruit a listening ear. Speaking about your board out loud can bring on some Aha! moments, which keeping your board under wraps doesn't. Their job is to listen and witness your thoughts, feelings and ideas. They might even write them down for you in a journal, in which you keep a record of your vision board conversations and the synchronistic outcomes.

Allow your listener the opportunity to express what they receive from your vision board too. But remember, your experience and your perceptions of your own vision board are primary. Foremost their feedback provides a useful comment about their anticipation of life through *your* board. You are not required to abide by their observations or interpretations, unless they resonate with you too.

7. Display

Treat your vision board with the respect it deserves by placing it in a prominent, elevated position. Let it sit. Glance at it from time to time and allow any impressions and inclinations to bubble to the surface. Chapter 7 goes through in detail how to explore your Intuitive Vision Board further and what you may discover on it.

I've made vision boards for 15 years now and when my daughter was young, she used to make her own with me. We'd display them over the kitchen table in our farmhouse cottage. In the morning while we were having breakfast, we'd take it in turns to talk about what was catching our attention that day and describe to each other what it was communicating to us, on our own boards and on each others'. It was an uplifting way to start the day and created connection, with the dog stretched out alongside the warm Aga with her ears half-cocked.

8. Act

You should know from what I've said earlier that making the Intuitive Vision Board can provoke strong feelings and be quite emotive for you. There is value in allowing your board to galvanise you into making changes. This may well include matters you have pushed to one side, not wanting to address or deeming them unimportant.

Don't let your hesitation however tip over into procrastination because at some point you'll be nudged into doing something – and if you don't, the nudge will become a push. Look what happened to me!

01: Initiation

02: Invocation

03: Invention

04: Inception

05: Immersion

06: Illumination

07: Integration

08: Inauguration

9. Repeat

I allow time every year to make a new Intuitive Vision Board. This is a good interval for you to have worked with and explored the various signs and symbols on your particular board. I use other expressive arts processes to stay connected to the unconscious dynamic coursing through my life such as the daily discipline of writing and drawing and attending natural movement workshops.

If you are experiencing a lot of change, you might be drawn to make the Intuitive Vision Board more often and that's perfectly acceptable too. It provides a reliable and comforting anchor when the outer circumstances of your life are changing rapidly.

Don'ts

Finally here are four things *not* to do when making the Intuitive Vision Board. We've touched on them all before but it's worth repeating them here.

Don't start reading

You may come across an article you want to read – but don't do this during the Intuitive Vision Board workshop because there just isn't time. As importantly, reading will snap you straight out of Remarkable-Right brain mode and back into Logical-Left that loves to know about things and devour information. If you come across something worth reading, just tear it out and put it to one side until after the creative process is complete.

Don't add a photo of yourself – or your loved ones

Placing a photograph of yourself – even one you like – in the centre is too literal and passé and is not in keeping with the spirit of the board. It's preferable instead that you find an image of someone who embodies the qualities you aspire to – but let it choose you and not you choose it. Perhaps there is something in the way they are conducting themselves that speaks volumes of how you would like to be or act. Or maybe they are dressed in a style you'd like to try out for yourself. These images are emotive and serving the purpose exactly as they are, so don't worry about the fact it isn't you in the photograph.

I'm often asked: *Shouldn't my children or partner be on here?* Of course you can add their photo later but this is counterintuitive. In any case, when you look closer, you may find they are already represented symbolically on your vision board such as dolphins playing in the water or puppies rolling in the grass.

If you've left off a photo of your partner or the two of you together as a couple – even a representational one – this is not an ominous sign. It could just mean your love relationship is integrated sufficiently into your life that it doesn't need to be on there; the vision board speaks more about the unmanifest future, not what exists already.

Don't add to the vision board later

Sometimes people ask me: *I didn't find an image of anyone that was suitable partner material, so is it okay to look for one and add it later?* I say ideally not. For whatever good reason, you didn't find one during the workshop yet you had ample opportunity to do so. You may jealously covet the images of gorgeous partners fellow creators found in their magazines. But you had the same choice of magazines and you didn't find them. Why is that?

Even though your Logical-Left is advising you to use the vision board opportunity to look for a partner and an image to represent them, it may not be your first priority and that's why the image did not appear. Perhaps there is something more important for you to take care of first that precludes you having a relationship right now. Writing this book was a perfect example for me; no images of relationship came to me during this time. Secondly, the image does not need to be literal so anything in twos could be symbolic of coupling and partnership. Those two elephants with their trunks entwined are already suggesting a love encounter.

Don't use words

Having recommended already you avoid using words on your vision board because they can switch on Logical-Left immediately, this next story shows how they can work implicitly through images, without the need to spell them out.

Homesick

I heard from a friend that someone was giving away a pile of magazines, which would be useful for my workshops. When I showed up at her door, it turned out to be a woman who had attended my Intuitive Vision Board workshop a year before. Now here she was space-clearing to leave home for another country and the magazines had to go.

I asked her where she was going. "South Africa," she said. "That doesn't surprise me at all," I replied, "because you had images of South Africa all over your last vision board. I remember it well because, when I pointed it out to you during the workshop, it brought tears to your eyes as it suddenly drove home to you how homesick you were."

Ironically, this woman also has the same initials as South Africa (SA). What's even funnier is that SA herself had forgotten all about the South African indicators on her Intuitive Vision Board, which had sat abandoned in the corner of her bedroom for the past 12 months. It was only when a friend came to help her pack and pointed it out to her that SA looked at her vision board again and there it all was.

In the interim the Intuitive Vision Board had brought SA's deeper needs to her attention one year earlier. Even when these needs slipped away from her conscious awareness, SA was already at work with them to manifest her vision anyway, without will or effort, gently prompted by the illustrations directing her towards the actions to take.

So now you have created the Intuitive Vision Board, we'll take a look in Chapter 6 – Illumination – at what the images might indicate.

"We are our own dark continent. Our own savage frontier."

Sarah Ban Breathnach, Author & Philanthropist

Chapter 6

ILLUMINATION

01: Initiation

02: Invocation

03: Invention

04: Inception

05: Immersion

06: Illumination

07: Integration

08: Inauguration

Precognition

Ideas, inspiration and visions are energetic life forms. They exist alright but they have no physical substance so we can't see them for looking, in the same way we can't see electricity but we know it is there. Conscious and determined, ideas are driven by a single impulse – to take form. However, this can only be achieved in cahoots with a human partner. So there they all are, these energetic, non-physical life forms, on the lookout for a promising suspect who has the inclination – and capability – to collaborate with them. Perhaps that can be you unless you are so preoccupied with the dramas of your day-to-day reality that you fail to even notice them. In which case, they may hover around you for a while before moving on to someone else who is more responsive to them.

Taking the time out to awaken your intuitive vision by making the Intuitive Vision Board sends out a signal that you are prepared to listen and are about to slip into receiver mode, just like the visionaries of old mentioned in Chapter 2. This is one very effective way to align your consciousness with universal intelligence and become a channel for creativity. Your intuitive vision then can no longer be a shopping list of goodies your ego is striving for but something that has already landed within your aura, wanting to cooperate with you. It is your destiny to do so, should you choose to accept this invitation.

Your intuitive vision is full of revelations and coincidences. In this chapter, we will take a closer look at the features of your finished Intuitive Vision Board and how to read the signs and symbols as counsel and foreknowledge of events to come.

Lightning rods

Symbols are like lightning rods. They can carry and transmute energy in ways that can serve us and create new pathways for us in the world. In contemplating the symbols on your Intuitive Vision Board, you are receptive to the possibility of changing your inner landscape and outer lifescape for the better – and consequently transforming your life. The challenge lies in sitting with the mystery posed by the symbols long enough for the wisdom to come to light, rather than chasing after answers in the customary way we believe is necessary to succeed.

01: Initiation

02: Invocation

03: Invention

04: Inception

05: Immersion

06: Illumination

07: Integration

08: Inauguration

Throughout the ages, even before vision boards were invented, people have read the signs as portents to prepare them for forthcoming events, even to avert disaster. So it was that predictions and premonitions came to pass. When you made the Intuitive Vision Board, your Remarkable-Right brain was turned on; you were in an expanded state of awareness and therefore operating beyond the limited frame of reference of your current identity. No matter how pleasant it was to be in this amplified waking dream-time, you can't remain there and get the washing-up done. The dream must come to an end but your vision doesn't need to and shouldn't. To separate from the vision and contemplate what it is all about requires you to shift out of dreamer and shift into observer mode.

The Intuitive Vision Board is a pastiche of ideas that belong together, by virtue of them coalescing in your psyche at a snapshot moment in time. This soulful gathering isn't arbitrary; it is unique to you. It holds the key to the particular combination of elements that both want to be associated with you and contribute to your highest good. I referred to it previously as both an emergence and a gestalt, which means your Intuitive Vision Board is a lot more than a collage of pretty pictures.

Its potential lies not with any one component part singled out in isolation but in the interrelationship of the parts to one another and to the whole, which gives it coherence. That's why I discourage you from going back to your Intuitive Vision Board and adding bits to it. By keeping within the time-frame allocated by the workshop, you maintain the integrity of the vision as communicated on the day. If you add to it later it will most likely be because your Logical-Left brain has convinced you that things are missing when in fact they aren't. The muse that had a hand in helping you to select the illustrations in the first place knows best and is holding the bigger picture.

When I work one-to-one with people after the workshop, my role is to help them unlock the deeper layers of meaning and allow the full significance of the board to unveil itself. In my absence, I will show you how to enquire of your Intuitive Vision Board to reveal the diamonds that may be hidden there. But first a further word about symbolism, because the images on your board are mostly symbolic not literal, intuitive not logical.

Signs and symbols

Symbols create a bridge between the realm of spirit and the realm of form. They also link seemingly disparate and diverse subject matter by their juxtaposition. These are associations you would never have made had you not awakened your intuitive vision and expressed the conversation you had with it on your Intuitive Vision Board.

The signs indicated are best read in the context of the person who has made the board and where they are on their life journey, and also in terms of the maker's historical and cultural background. For instance, the symbolic colour of mourning is black to Westerners and white to the Chinese. You can expect to find yourself relating to a symbol on your terms, although you may want to research further for additional meaning.

Symbols open doors to our subconscious, unconscious and superconscious realities which would otherwise remain closed. Carl Jung regarded the symbol as the psychological mechanism by which energy and states of mind are transformed into material form, without us needing to analyse why or even to be aware of this while it is happening; it is enough that the symbol exists in your conscious awareness. You may only ever come to appreciate the foreknowledge of the sign that appeared retrospectively and if you try too hard to dissect it while it's in process, the benefits may elude you.

Signs and symbols fall into two broad categories:

1. Messenger signs

These convey important information and guidance for your well-being. It is not essential that they are show-stopping in appearance. They can also include much softer prods in the direction you need to go to be more authentic and bring more balance to your life.

2. Shadow signs

Occasionally, when a negative psychological pattern is about to reoccur, it may show its face first on your vision board. Some people regard this as negative. I don't. I say thank you. Here is an opportunity to resolve an old issue that is presenting itself once again because it is potentially blocking your progress while it remains. Besides, I have never seen a negative omen appear on an Intuitive Vision Board.

01: Initiation

02: Invocation

03: Invention

04: Inception

05: Immersion

06: Illumination

07: Integration

08: Inauguration

Symbols are openings to new potentialities. I can't emphasise this enough. Your Intuitive Vision Board seldom contains visual representations of your most important life goals: "This is the house I'm going to live in one day, full stop!" "This is the car I want to drive, done deal!" "This is the person I plan to marry, game over!" So when it comes to deciphering their meaning you must rely less on deduction and more on your intuition and contextual reasoning. It is only by keeping the conversation open and not jumping straight to conclusions, which can stop you listening further, that the full implication of the sign will be exposed. Each is a gift to be treasured. To embrace them all is to receive the abundance waiting for you and all your heart's desire.

It is unlikely you will take hold of the big picture on the day you make your Intuitive Vision Board. I've never known this to happen. It's more likely you will glance across one day and gasp. What has emerged in the interim can represent a sea change in your thinking and a significant turnaround in the wheel of your life.

The Intuitive Vision Board is very smart and highly selective: it cuts through the myriad of choices a materially abundant lifestyle can tempt you with and that can paralyse you from making a wise decision. It will already have separated out the hankerings of the ego and used discernment to focus on what you need most to create a meaningful life. It is a veritable road map, and the very act of creating it has woven a web of interconnecting psychic energy and the magic will have begun – as Joanna's next story vividly demonstrates.

Synchronicity moves house and county

By the time Joanna made her Intuitive Vision Board she and her husband had already decided they were going to up sticks and move to the West Country. However, there were three big hurdles to overcome which she couldn't get her head around. First, her husband was still in full-time employment. Second, they had yet to put their house on the market – and sell it. Third, they had not even begun to look for a new home.

On Joanna's vision board there were two images of grandiose houses with extensive landscaped gardens and high-chiselled hedges like in a maze. "I don't know what that's all about," she'd said, "we'll never be able to afford a place like that." Right in the centre were two penguins walking together through Northern American scenery. "That's my husband and I," she told me. "We hope to travel when he retires."

Eight months later I visited her in Cornwall. I was there to witness how they had pulled the whole vision off. All of the features I'm about to describe, down to the last detail, were featured on the board she made *eight months earlier* – including the grandiose house with the high-chiselled hedges.

Joanna walked me through extensive terraced gardens with secret hideaways, every turn revealing yet another bird table. All of this situated on their own private hillside that cascaded down to a stream at its base, among tall trees that would be carpeted with daffodils and bluebells in the springtime. As darkness descended we retreated into a spacious lounge inside the stone-clad house with the woodburning stove. *All of this and more had featured on her vision board.*

Joanna could hardly contain her excitement as she described the off-white kitchen that was being installed three days later. How did she know eight months earlier that her new place would require an off-white kitchen before she'd even found the home? We smiled together at the image of the elephant dancing upside down on a toilet on one hand on her board as she pointed out the *five toilets* in their new home. An elephant is a symbol of abundance. How many people do you know with five toilets in their family home?

What had transpired for this couple in the interim?

Within four months of making her vision board Joanna's husband had the opportunity to retire with a settlement package. Immediately the couple shot down to the West Country for a week and found their dream home. It had been waiting empty for them for two years. On their return, they put their house on the market, it sold quickly, and they relocated westwards with lightning speed.

One month after moving in they flew to Canada. They walked through mountainous scenery and along driftwood beaches just like the ones on Joanna's board. They stayed in their son's timber-framed property surrounded by forest, exactly as she'd illustrated. Her son had even positioned a row of coloured vases on a high beam to catch the light, similar to the line of coloured vases in the centre of Joanna's vision board. How is that even possible? It is and it was.

01: Initiation
02: Invocation
03: Invention
04: Inception
05: Immersion
06: Illumination
07: Integration
08: Inauguration

Placement

Once the Intuitive Vision Board is finished, place it in a prominent position where you can look at it easily at eye level. From a Feng Shui perspective, I recommend a spot where there is plenty of light and the chi can flow freely and unobstructed. Two favoured locations are in the bedroom or over your desk. Don't hide your board in a cupboard where energy can't circulate, for example. Or in the boot of your car, where one maker left hers and allowed her family to dump their stuff all over it, a perfect metaphor for how they behaved towards her generally. Treat your Intuitive Vision Board with the respect it deserves, holding all that rich potential in waiting for you.

Glance at your board from time to time. This alone should be enough to trigger your unconscious; it shouldn't require effort, willpower or affirmations. Then stay alert to the synchronistic signs as they arise and commit to acting upon them. This may require you to step out of your comfort zone and do something you wouldn't normally do. Or embrace something unusual happening, rather than beat a hasty retreat or paper over it. Don't be too quick to judge events as either positive or negative; flow with these nudges, because the unexpected and the unanticipated can change your whole game-plan in an instant.

How to approach your finished board

Now it's the sixty-four thousand dollar question. What does it all mean?

Before you launch into analysis, please allow me to hold you back one moment longer. I want to prepare you for making friends with your new board in the same way you prepared yourself to awaken your intuition before making the board itself.

Quality time

Set aside unflustered time to sit with your new friend, occasionally. Be still and wait. Allow your attention to be both curious and welcoming. Set aside any preconceived ideas about what you are looking for or recalling what you may have noticed before. Allow fresh impressions to come to you. An image once birthed (as an individual image or the entire vision board) has a life of its own. You need to give it time to make itself known to you and give yourself time to become familiar with it.

01: Initiation

02: Invocation

03: Invention

04: Inception

05: Immersion

06: Illumination

07: Integration

08: Inauguration

Use imagination

Rather than treating the signs and symbols in a detached, rational way, which keeps you at a distance and gets in the way of any burgeoning intimacy, experiment with allowing your imagination free rein. Images are powerful because they can hold the key to what you know already at a deep level but cannot yet describe in words. Let the images encourage you to perceive things differently – about yourself and your life in general – drawing you out of your comfortable shell and enabling you to connect with a wider field of possibility.

Question

You may start by selecting one image that calls out for your attention. Describe: What do you see? What are you feeling? What does it suggest to you – or remind you of? Where is it located in relation to other images? Let any musings, associations, memories emerge without force. Ask yourself then: "What might I do with this information?" Don't expect the answers to come right away. Just leave them floating and they will surely arrive at the appropriate moment.

Be surprised

You may recognise some images as personal favourites. But don't jump to conclusions just yet because this might preclude a further twist in the tale emerging. Conversely you may find yourself looking at a picture which is completely unfamiliar and mysterious. Welcome these strangers into your life and allow them a bit longer to reveal why they have made their appearance now.

The wisdom of your Intuitive Vision Board will take time to unfold. Stay interested and engaged with it as it steers you in the direction of what you might do to promote your one wild and wonderful life.

01: Initiation

02: Invocation

03: Invention

04: Inception

05: Immersion

06: Illumination

07: Integration

08: Inauguration

Understanding your
Intuitive Vision Board

Now you are ready. What does it all mean? Here are 12 awesome indications of what might have appeared on your Intuitive Vision Board.

At the end of this chapter there is space for you to record your observations. I suggest you record your thoughts the day after making your board and then again at least six months later:

1. Reminders

Is there something you've been putting off doing, which you've talked about for ages, waiting for the perfect moment? If it has appeared on your board you are being prompted to do something about it now. Trust that the time and money to enable this will take care of themselves and you'll gain a lot more besides. Logical-Left may try to convince you that this is just a diversion from the main show. Don't be convinced. There may be more at stake than you think and some interesting synchronicity is ready to occur. Besides, the joy that comes from engaging with these activities could generate sparks of vitality to ignite other areas of your life in need of rejuvenation.

2. Synchronicity

Synchronicity was a term originally coined by Carl Jung. It describes the juxtaposition of events and experiences that previously had no causal link to one another. In conjoining now they create new meaning to guide you in a particular direction, because there is no such thing as a random coincidence.

Synchronicity can be about people, places and situations we attract into our life to help us. Their occurrence can herald a game-changing moment but you may not realise it at the time. An indication that synchronicity is about to occur can show up on your Intuitive Vision Board because your intuition is in correspondence with universal intelligence. Staying alert to this possibility and showing a willingness to participate in it, with wonder and awe, will encourage the frequency of these happenings.

3. Solutions

In constructing your vision board you may inadvertently have constellated the solution to a problem. Or you may have uncovered a problem you didn't realise you had, but now you've brought both the problem and the answer into the light of day. How clever is your Remarkable-Right brain, quietly at work on your behalf. It has the ability to take a helicopter view of the complete terrain and spot any patterns present in a way that Logical-Left can't.

4. Precognition

Sometimes specific items appear on your Intuitive Vision Board and you literally find yourself buying, receiving or visiting them. Their size is immaterial and can range in scale from a wedding ring to a house. You could say that once it's appeared on your vision board, your subconscious is going to prompt you every time you look at it to search it out. But why those things in the first place? That's the mystery of it.

I went to work in Latvia once and had a full day to explore Riga. I wandered around a shopping mall where I bought a pair of knee-length leather boots. Then I visited an outdoors market where I bought a burnt-orange cloche hat. To my amazement both these items, down to the exact colour and style, were already pictured on my vision board back home. On the same vision board, I'd placed a beautiful large, white house designed in a way to allow light to filter in from all sides. The architectural style was very distinctive and I'd made a mental note it was in Sweden and there was snow on the ground.

Three months later I'm on a plane to Stockholm to do a Feng Shui consultation, which had not been planned when I made my board. When the job was over, my client took me on a city tour, which included a visit to a property similar in size and design to the beautiful one on my vision board. It was February and everywhere there was snow on the ground.

5. People

People and animals are associated with the energy of the heart, love and the need for connection. When these appear on your vision board it may indicate your desire for more contact and of a particular type, depending on the character of the person portrayed or the nature of the animal. If you don't have any people or animals, the converse may be true. You need more alone time to be with yourself. As with all the signs and symbols appearing, they are neither good nor bad; they are useful information for you.

01: Initiation

02: Invocation

03: Invention

04: Inception

05: Immersion

06: Illumination

07: Integration

08: Inauguration

As I said earlier, I don't advocate putting a photograph of yourself in the middle of your board. It limits you to a memory of who you have been rather than who you are becoming. The connotations are too literal and it doesn't allow for qualities or attributes you might intuitively wish to acquire or develop. An image of a stranger you've chosen randomly may embody your aspirations better and convey a presence you wish to emulate.

I once made a board which contained large, evocative images of three very different women. Through their body language and style of dress they each depicted aspects I wished to cultivate in myself but had not recognised prior to making the vision board.

The appearance of someone on your board can also imply that person is about to enter your life. I once cut out a photograph of a young man. I fantasised he looked creative with IT skills and was working for me, so I nicknamed him Man Friday. Until then I had not considered employing anyone but a week later, tearing my hair out at the computer, I decided to seek help. My advertisement read: "Wanted. Man Friday". The first person to respond was actually a young man who did some ad hoc work for me. The second person offered herself to me as a Woman Friday – and she has been working with me ever since.

6. Animals and birds

Animals, birds and other creatures always appear on vision boards. Nature symbols represent archetypal energy we can call upon to aid us rather like a totem or a power animal. Birds, associated with the element of air, are often ancient symbols of the soul and our spiritual nature. They can signify awakening to new ideas or an increase in intellectual ability, while animals represent our more instinctual nature. Shamans remind us that animals speak to those who listen and trees have messages for us when we are quiet.

An animal appearing on your board can sometimes represent someone about to come into your life with those instinctual characteristics. I once cut out an image of a women wearing a cowboy hat very similar to the one I owned when I was her age. Behind her I'd placed a large sea otter that towered over her in a protective way, which suggested to me it was a "he" and he was covering her back.

At one time in my life, before I started a family, I visited the west coast of America three times, including for my Feng Shui training. I developed an affinity for sea otters after watching them initially in the maritime museum in Monterey and then encountering them in the wild (described in the section on animal totems in Chapter 4). During the reign of my cowboy hat/sea otter vision board, a tall man came into my life – a chance encounter. He acted on my behalf, immediately covered my back and helped to extract me from a difficult situation. I later discovered he'd grown up on the west coast of America and Monterey in particular. Mr Sea Otter I've nicknamed him.

7. Colours

Colour is energy which vibrates at different frequencies. The warmer colours are more energetic while the cooler colours have a slower vibration. It's not all in the imagination either because some blind people can actually feel the difference between the colours. Your vision board is filled with colour and, by reflecting on what colours predominate, can inform you. Similarly, the colour you've associated with your animal totem may indicate the type of energy you need more of.

Colour corresponds to the different energy centres in the body called chakras. The job of a chakra is to store, balance and redistribute energy. By relating the colours on your vision board to the chakras you might learn about what your body needs to support your well-being. Each person has their own cultural vocabulary when it comes to colour; therefore it's best to see what associations come to you first, before you cross-reference to a colour system like the simple one below.

> » Crown Chakra (**Purple or White**): spirituality, enlightenment and connection to Source
> » Third Eye Chakra (**Indigo/Very Dark Blue**): intuition, dreams, psychic ability
> » Throat Chakra (**Mid Blue or Turquoise**): communication, speaking, listening
> » Heart Chakra (**Green or Pink**): love, nurturing, relationship
> » Naval Chakra (**Yellow**): power, will, determination
> » Sacral Chakra (**Orange**): sexuality, creativity, joy
> » Root Chakra (**Red, Brown, Black or Grey**): survival, protection, being grounded

8. Numbers

When numbers appear on your vision board it could signify the precognition of a literal occurrence, such as the number of the next house you might purchase; I've known this to happen many times. It is also worth noting the number of times a motif repeats itself, such as the number of beds or the number of beaches.

On my current board I have a numerical sequence of 1 to 8 presented in a decorative way. It just so happens there are eight chapters to my book. On the same board, the number 7 reoccurs three times and the numerology of the IBSN number of this book also reduces down to a 7. In terms of the Enneagram, 7 is the number of my "enthusiastic visionary",

97

01: Initiation

02: Invocation

03: Invention

04: Inception

05: Immersion

06: Illumination

07: Integration

08: Inauguration

quite an appropriate personality type to be writing this book, don't you think? The Enneagram, in case you're wondering, is an ancient tool for self-understanding based on nine distinct personality types.

Numbers have energetic qualities in the way colours do and it's the study of their resonance that forms the basis of numerology. Here are some simple definitions:

1 – **Unity** – the individual, beginnings, leadership.
2 – **Differentiation** – Also harmonious coupling – marriage or partnership.
3 – **Creativity** – vitality, motion and dynamic process.
4 – **Foundation** – grounding, boundaries, structure.
5 – **Physical** – in the body and in nature, activity. Change.
6 – **Creativity** – perfection, equilibrium. Deepening of spirituality.
7 – **Mysticism** – alchemy and illumination. Ambition achieved.
8 – **Stability** – rebirth and abundance. Harmony of opposites.
9 – **Synthesis** – harvesting of resources, completion.
10 – **Unity** – God. Visual representation of male and female.
11 – **A master number** – intuition, creativity, genius, refinement.
12 – **Cosmic order** – 12 signs of the zodiac. 12 months in a year.

9. Shapes

"The Universal Shape Theory" was so-named by anthropologist Angeles Arrien. Cross-culturally she identified five basic shapes, which have appeared in art throughout the ages, yet worldwide people have ascribed similar meanings to them: the circle, the square, the triangle, the cross and the spiral. Your Intuitive Vision Board is full of shapes, some of which you've cut out yourself while the rest are an integral part of the images you have chosen. It's worth reflecting on what this might mean for you.

Circle – for wholeness and individuation.
Square – for stability, solidity and foundations.
Triangle – for goals, dreams and visions.
Cross – for relationship, balancing and integration.
Spiral – for growth, evolution and change.

10. Movement and direction

It's not as if the vision board creator sets out with this in mind but some boards show an overall pattern of movement to them. Or the eye is drawn to travel across the board

01: Initiation

02: Invocation

03: Invention

04: Inception

05: Immersion

06: Illumination

07: Integration

08: Inauguration

in a certain way. Where does yours start? Where does yours finish? Which direction is it moving in? These are good questions to reflect on.

The image – or set of images – occupying the central position are always pertinent. They can often hold the overall theme or purpose to this particular vision board. Your eyes will always be drawn to the centre and the rest of the board can hinge around what is happening there. If your board does not have an obvious centre to it, that doesn't matter either. It's not essential.

In the centre of my current board I have a vivid blue photograph of the Blue Mountains in NSW, Australia. They are so-named because the vast forests of eucalyptus give off a hazy mist in the hot sun, which looks blue from a distance. I have never been to Australia so time will tell whether this literally comes true. Meanwhile the blue is vast and deep and is a constant reminder to me to empty my mind of thoughts and expand my energy field in service of my intuitive ability. On all four sides of the Blue Mountains on my board there are animals and birds noted for their extrasensory intelligence; they have a distinctive hearing apparatus or special antennae for that. Again this prompts me to wait and listen for the messages and look out for signs I might receive *out of the blue*. There's a photograph of the vision board to which I'm referring on the front cover of the book and some of the creatures are illustrated at the start of the chapters.

11. Space

With so much choice available of things to do and places to go, it is very tempting to fill every available minute with activity – and this often plays out on your Intuitive Vision Board. Some makers fill every inch with overlapping images, even hanging off the side. A man once covered both sides of his board in a frenetic haste and then asked for another with which to do the same thing. There is nothing wrong with this; making your Intuitive Vision Board is an embodied therapeutic process, which means how you approach making it is worthy of consideration in itself.

You may have lots of space between images with nothing overlapping. Or a mixture of the two. This can change for you from board to board. I once watched a woman paste down two images only, the size of postage stamps, during the entire workshop. That was until the very last minute. When I looked across again she'd added a huge fox, which I found most revealing. Paradoxically, the key symbolic notes of fox are to do with camouflage, shape-shifting and invisibility.

At the end of his workshop, William had only filled one half of his board. The images were travelling, horizontally and methodically, across his vision board, from right to

99

01: Initiation

02: Invocation

03: Invention

04: Inception

05: Immersion

06: Illumination

07: Integration

08: Inauguration

left. William was a bit disgruntled because he felt he hadn't finished it and his board was incomplete. I felt the opposite; it was expressing a truth in waiting and it was perfect exactly as he'd left it.

The distinct edge of the images reminded me of the prow of a big ship, steaming ahead into the vastness of the ocean (the empty remaining space on his board). I had the impression of something yet to be discovered in the uncharted waters ahead and wondered if he needed to take his foot off the pedal to allow whatever it was to break through.

It was several months later before I heard from William that his small business had developed radically. No longer a sole trader, he had created a limited company and a whole new arm to his enterprise with a virtual team to implement it. I believe this was the reason why he needed to leave so much empty space on his vision board for him to sail into it.

12. Shadow

I sometimes get asked whether negative things appear on the Intuitive Vision Board. I touched on this earlier in the chapter. Having watched many boards being made my answer is no and anyway our perception is always our choice. It's true I've witnessed people feeling ambivalent about the images they'd chosen. However, if there was still some attraction, I would always encourage the image(s) to remain to see where they led the maker, as this next story demonstrates.

What's not being said speaks up on the vision board

I was invited to facilitate three directors of a company, each to produce their own Intuitive Vision Board in a workshop I ran especially for them. I coached them afterwards as a team. Two of the three had strong and large eruptive images on their board. One of these images permeated the entire backdrop, while the other had an arrow-like image shooting upwards from the baseline. The third board had nothing of this sort on it at all.

There was no obvious explanation for these eruptions at the time and we left it at that. Three months later the relationship between the three partners exploded unexpectedly, resulting in one of them quitting the business while the two remaining were left reeling. Retrospectively you could point to the aforementioned images on their boards as negative portents. Or you could re-perceive these images as a significant sign that something needed to surface, explode and dissipate to enable the company to become stronger and organise itself differently for growth. Besides there is every possibility the third had already entertained the idea of leaving and had not yet said anything but the other two had picked this up intuitively for it to appear on their boards.

When something that isn't so pretty appears on the vision board, I encourage the creator to rejoice. It may have a darker connotation and point towards the shadow. But just because it's negative doesn't mean it should be censored. Images are ambivalent. If it's an obstacle to be encountered then best not to fight it but find a way around it or transmute the energy into something that is more useful.

In Chapter 7 – Integration – we will explore how you can integrate the signs and symbols you have received on your Intuitive Vision Board into your life. Meanwhile, you can record your discoveries on the chart below.

Intuitive Vision Board Readings

DATE MADE:	NEW-BORN VISION	6 MONTHS LATER	NOTES
Reminders			
Synchronicity			
Solutions			
Precognition			
People			
Animals & Birds			
Colours			
Numbers			
Shapes			
Movement & Direction			
Space			
Shadow			

01: Initiation
02: Invocation
03: Invention
04: Inception
05: Immersion
06: Illumination
07: Integration
08: Inauguration

01: Initiation

02: Invocation

03: Invention

04: Inception

05: Immersion

06: Illumination

07: Integration

08: Inauguration

01: Initiation

02: Invocation

03: Invention

04: Inception

05: Immersion

06: Illumination

07: Integration

08: Inauguration

*"All you have is within you, all that your heart desires,
all that your nature so specially fits you for – that or the
counterpart of it waits embedded in the great whole..."*

Edward Carpenter, Poet

Chapter 7

INTEGRATION

On a grave note...

Out walking the dog early one morning, I find myself in a graveyard admiring the colours of the tombstones bathed in the soft light of the morning. I lift my gaze to beyond the railings in the distance and the commuters – a sinuous, unbroken line of black cars, queuing for the white ornate bridge, which allows only one or two to cross at a time. The cars resemble a funeral procession, while their drivers will barely notice the bridge – or the magnificent weir spanning the Thames. Their attention is fixated on getting to the other side as quickly as possible to beat a hasty escape from Marlow. First settled in the Bronze Age and with Georgian buildings still standing, the town has everything you could ever wish for within walking distance. The bridge was built by civil engineer William Tierney Clark, who also built the Széchenyi Chain Bridge in Budapest, which spans the river Danube. Both towns and bridges are stunning.

My gaze returns to the gravestones in the foreground, also in a line. They call to mind something which has remained with me always, the number one regret of dying people in their last few days of life, as recorded by a palliative care nurse in a study she had undertaken:

"I wish I'd had the courage to live a life true to myself not the life others expected of me."

When people realise their life is almost over and look back on it with such clarity, it's painful to see how many dreams have gone unattended while they were busy fulfilling other agendas they had not consciously chosen for themselves. Perhaps they also succumbed to social pressure that measures success in one dimension only, like my father did: "How much wealth do you have?" This has so little to do with how many lives you have touched, how much love you gave to those around you, or whether you were indeed able to discover and live your vocation.

I thought again of the black cars queuing in a line and wondered how many of the drivers had the experience of meaning and purpose to their lives. It must be excruciating to die knowing your life was the consequence of choices made and compromises accepted along the way – and these were not what you would have chosen. Then finally to realise you can't take the money, the cars, the properties, the holidays with you.

So what legacy will you leave behind, what footprint in the sand?

One wild and wonderful life

I ran a survey in the process of writing. I wanted to hear first-hand what it was that readers might be concerned about that could be addressed in the book. The overarching question was: "Are you making the most of your one wild and wonderful life?" The majority of responders said "no" and the top three reasons given were:

» **Time.** Not enough of it. Confusion over how to prioritise conflicting demands.
» **Mindset.** The confidence to take a stand for what they wanted instead.
» **Money.** Not enough of it left over after home/family commitments were accounted for.

I was sad to hear this but glad it was being voiced, because there was more chance it would bring the people one step closer to addressing their predicament. On the other hand, their answers didn't surprise me. I know how easy it is to get stuck on the treadmill, driven by a one-track mind and days that pass all too quickly. However, by continuing to do nothing about it, they will remain on the path of regret and the sentiment expressed by dying people.

Why is it then we have more wherewithal than ever before but lack the courage to do something with it?

The fact that you've already got this far into the book tells me you have both the willingness and the desire to take a self-reflective step backwards. That overworked Logical-Left brain that thinks it has all the answers will run away with itself if you allow it. However, it is not equipped to address a complex problem like knowing what it is you *really* need to lead a deeply meaningful life while also paying the bills. Remarkable-Right brain is much better suited to addressing this and fortunately you have access to one of these too. But first you must slow things down, clear your mind, settle into your body – all those conditions you've seen Remarkable-Right adores in order for creativity to ripen and flourish. In this frame of mind you are fit to participate in the creative meditation offered by the Intuitive Vision Board. Exploring the deeper layers of consciousness in an awake dream state, ideas and possibilities previously unavailable can now announce themselves to you.

The genius that is communicating with you through the images chosen can literally set you off on an alternative life trajectory, if you allow it. Just be mindful that Logical-Left doesn't try to intercede and justify why it makes no sense to be awakening your intuitive

01: Initiation

02: Invocation

03: Invention

04: Inception

05: Immersion

06: Illumination

07: Integration

08: Inauguration

vision right now. This is the equivalent to standing on a snail; in an instant it shatters and all that juicy life force escapes and dries out. Then where are you? Back to square one. Directionless, anchorless, and struggling to find the courage and conviction to live true to yourself.

Why are we derailed so easily?

I believe this is due to the widespread cultural phenomenon of the last two centuries referred to as the existential vacuum. More people have more wealth than ever before – and some excessively so – but we still struggle to ascribe purpose to our lives. For many, creating wealth means working hard all week to achieve it – not just the person going out to do the job but also the person behind the scenes who manages the facility (the home), nurtures the talent (the children), and caters for everyone's needs besides food. It's because of this we feel we deserve a reward because fulfilment from the job alone is not enough.

Then we have a tendency to be greedy and overindulge in food, drink, holidays and buying stuff to satiate our needs yet it is also possible to have too much of a good thing. At the same time we are too scared to relinquish any of the excess we've built up around us like a fortress, feeling too vulnerable without it while being unprepared to explore the alternatives. Locked up inside our Logical-Left thinking, we've lost the connection to what we truly value and our natural instincts, which would tell us what to resist and what to fight for.

Pain avoidance

The problem is perpetuated by an unspoken ground rule that we must avoid discomfort and sacrifice at any cost yet the reality is that life will throw us unavoidable curveballs anyway. We have grown accustomed to living with a pathological fear of pain and believing any form of difficulty should be avoided like the plague. Believing these thoughts to be true turns us into a pride of scaredy cats, unwilling to take risks that might upset the status quo or embark on an adventure without sight of the land ahead. While expending good effort in our attempts to avoid perceived danger, we create a different version of it, as the dying people so clearly understood:

01: Initiation

02: Invocation

03: Invention

04: Inception

05: Immersion

06: Illumination

07: Integration

08: Inauguration

"I wish I'd had the courage to live a life true to myself not the life others expected of me."

There is a natural ebb and flow to life, gain and loss, rough with the smooth. It's our destiny as human beings to experience suffering and, as a consequence, grow wiser, become more loving and learn resilience. If our overriding motivation is to live in a stress-free zone, we eliminate the creative tension that is generated by strife and wrestling with a worthwhile goal and a seemingly insurmountable task. The struggle alone can generate a huge amount of energy and propel us into a new playing field entirely. Compare this with living in an empty existential vacuum. Which do you gravitate towards? Making an Intuitive Vision Board can help you choose wisely.

Passion and purpose

Viktor Frankl in his seminal book *Man's Search for Meaning* writes so clearly about passion and purpose from his experience. The only way to survive the horrors of Auschwitz and the German prisoner of war camps was to find meaning in the most miserable of circumstances we could ever imagine. Each moment they faced the choice to opt out and become the plaything of circumstance or to opt in by taking up their cross and bearing it with dignity. Besides, the hardship endured can become an asset for the future. We should never give up hope because we don't know the whole story yet. It's worth observing that Viktor Frankl led by example. Not only did he survive the prisoner of war camps, but he also proceeded to reach over 10 million people worldwide with his message.

I believe everyone is born with a special purpose for being here. I believe there is a much greater intelligence, beyond the individual's, shaping the world – and all the other worlds in the galaxies. I also believe it's in our interests to get in tune with this greater intelligence and one way to do this is by making your Intuitive Vision Board. Your job is to discover what your individual assignment is – and then to run with it. So many of us would fare much better knowing what the something was to live for or the someone for whom we would go to the edge for. Without passion and commitment to contain us, our lives can become flabby and ironically lifeless.

Happiness

Where to look to comprehend the consequences of remaining on the path of complacency and avoiding the road to fulfilment?

The ancient Greeks made a useful distinction between short- and long-term happiness. When considering both they believed it necessary to distinguish between two types of motivation and rewards. The first is *hedonistic* – the drive for pleasure-seeking and to minimise discomfort. The focus is on attaining short-term goals like a good night out, signing up the dream job, or the engagement ring on the finger – and our lives can tend to organise mostly around these activities. Epicurus was big on hedonism; he pursued a life devoted to sensual pleasure (epicurean tastes). But the downside of investing in short-term happiness alone is it's not sustainable; there is always a comedown after the high, which we explored in Chapter 2 with reference to the difference between an intuitive vision and a strategic goal-setting exercise that uses pictures.

The alternative drive for long-term happiness is towards *eudaimonia*, which we also touched on earlier. This is motivated by a desire to discover your place in the world and to feel part of something greater than yourself. Aristotle was an advocate of eudaimonia. He believed the highest levels of achievement were attained by striving to express the best that is within you as opposed to satisfying personal appetite. Your first call should be to consider eudaimonia because the peace and contentment that accompanies long-term happiness can help you to survive the mood swings of life and hedonistic delights which come and go. It's also the case that when you are engaged in eudaimonic endeavours, you enjoy peak experiences; artists and athletes in particular report that when engrossed in what they are doing, they are in a state of flow and linear time ceases to exist.

Short-term and long-term happiness are different phenomena and experienced in the two different halves of the brain, left and right respectively. The more evident in contemporary culture is the drive towards short-term hedonistic happiness, which some attain to their detriment while others constantly strive for it with random success. Without eudaimonic motivation to balance us out, we won't come close to self-actualisation and must take responsibility for this now. The Intuitive Vision Board is such a good tool for this very purpose and is why creating a board is an act of maturity. The people, places and activities that instil more eudaimonic value will become evident to you while the more traditional entitlement vision board will limit you to hedonistic goals that won't lead you anywhere you don't know already.

Down to earth

How can we use the concepts of hedonistic and eudaimonic on a day-to-day basis? I like Elizabeth Gilbert's pragmatic approach. She makes a useful distinction between job, career, hobby and vocation – reminding us they are four different words with four different meanings. Since you may find indications of these on your Intuitive Vision Board at different times, it's useful to distinguish between them to understand their respective value. I have taken this one step further and associated each with a hedonistic or eudaimonic motivation.

Job ~ Hedonistic

Everyone needs one of these to survive and pay the bills. Even if your work is unpaid (as when you manage the home and raise the children or when you are a volunteer), you are still dependent on someone who has a job unless you have another income stream. A job doesn't need to carry an awesome title or be particularly fulfilling and it can be done on a full or part-time basis. You simply need to be able to serve in a way that people want and you get paid for.

Once over the initial shock of my decline and fall described in Chapter 1, I found the Intuitive Vision Board, made nine months earlier, indicated exactly the right job to suit my needs. I didn't even know such a product existed or that there would be work for me for me in selling these floatation rooms, let alone ten minutes' drive from my home. But my vision board did – and this job proved to be a godsend. The contact with people in the well-being industry all over the world helped me to feel less isolated with my difficulties. It fitted in with the school run. It paid the bills and also allowed me to recommence my own vocational work out of hours.

Similarly, as I write this book, I am doing a full-time job covering a maternity leave in a solicitor's practice. I work with a team of 20 fun and intelligent people and the daily contact feeds me while I complete the solitary task of writing at the weekends and in the holidays. As I work with the designer and editor to get this book ready to print, I have changed jobs yet again and I am now selling houses part-time, which fits nicely alongside my Feng Shui skills.

Career ~ Hedonistic

A career usually pays more than a job. A job turns into a career when you are dedicated to what you are doing. Or there is some kind of development path for you in it and you are willing to put in extra hours without overtime pay. To continue with a career that takes up so much time and is not moving you towards a bigger goal is self-destructive and perhaps you need to extract yourself from there.

01: Initiation

02: Invocation

03: Invention

04: Inception

05: Immersion

06: Illumination

07: Integration

08: Inauguration

Hobby ~ Eudaimonic

This activity is pursued purely for joy and delight. There is no need to generate income from it or even to become the best you can possibly be at it. I like to think of the hobby as the great enabler.

Dance is a good example for me. Because I am a natural dancer, I've sometimes confused this with believing I needed to make a career out of it by teaching professionally and I have obtained the highest teaching qualification in it. Yet I've discovered this is not the case. I need to dance for myself first and foremost. When I express myself in movement, it enlivens me and switches on my creativity, which has a knock-on effect in all areas of my life. When things are not going swimmingly well and I'm becoming a bit cranky, I know it's time for me to go dancing. What hobby might do this for you?

Vocation ~ Eudaimonic

This includes any activity you feel *called* to do, even when you don't feel like doing anything else. Even when you know you might fail and are unlikely to gain worldwide recognition from it. It might at first appear to be quite an unremarkable activity you are drawn to do. But a vocation is nevertheless compelling and it won't let you go so easily. No matter how difficult it seems to pursue it, somehow you must because it's the way you make your unique contribution to the whole and leave your mark on the world. You are like Cinderella and this shoe fits your foot only. In time other people may come to recognise this about you too and respect you for it but this is not what motivates you.

Why more of us don't seek out our vocation and therefore settle for less returns us to the two halves of the brain discussion. When we're locked up inside Logical-Left we use only a small portion of our available intelligence for important decisions like these. To engage with the vaster sea of intelligence, we need to unlock the much greater capacity afforded by our dormant Remarkable-Right to awaken our intuition and let rip on the Intuitive Vision Board.

There was an older woman who was living in my town well past retirement age. She was in charge of bookings for a prominent church hall and some found her a little intimidating to deal with because she insisted on doing things properly. As an environmentalist and activist in the Transition Town movement, she cycled everywhere on a push bike. She volunteered weekly in the local museum and in her quiet, unflamboyant style she was a pillar of local society in contrast to the more affluent displays of it in this wealthy town. None of the many ways in which she contributed were paid for. And when she died everyone missed her and many, beyond her family, came to honour her at the funeral,

111

01: Initiation

02: Invocation

03: Invention

04: Inception

05: Immersion

06: Illumination

07: Integration

08: Inauguration

passing by the very same gravestones I mentioned earlier in this chapter. This woman had found her vocation and what she stood for – and was devoted to living it.

Calling

We can all have a vocation – something that calls to us both as individuals and as organisations. It answers the "why am I here?" question and shows us how we are uniquely placed to serve using our particular combination of character, personality, skills and attributes. Martin Seligman, of Positive Psychology, talks about using our signature strengths to escape the Monday to Friday treadmill to find our true calling.

Our personal calling is always synchronised with universal intelligence and that's how we become our most potent. From my own experience and of working with others, your calling can take years to evolve and become evident. Elements of it will find you when you least expect it. All you can do in the interim is prepare for its arrival by staying close to what's in your heart. And one tool that readily enables this is the Intuitive Vision Board.

These callings – and our willingness to respond to them – occur more often than we realise. We are drawn to a person, a situation, a place without knowing why. When I reflect on the punctuation points in my career – from the 18-year-old choosing to study Anthropology at university, considered marginal at the time, to the various types of work that have been the stepping stones of my career ever since, I'm shocked to discover that I didn't plan any of them. My circumstances were such that neither parent was involved with my decisions, so I learned to roll with my hunches early on. Some invisible muse must have been charting my course and I was sufficiently open to go with it; I didn't need to know what the end-destination would look like or who I would become.

We don't know the whole story yet

However, one gentle nudge from your Intuitive Vision Board is unlikely to be enough to propel you to your final destination in one go. This means you will have to let go of the handrail without knowing where you will end up. While if you continue to grip the handrail, you will prevent yourself from moving at all. A leap of faith is required to take that first step, while it's reassuring to know there is never a right or wrong move. And remember the next step after that will only become clear once you've set off, if you recall that quote attributed to Goethe: "What you can do or dream you can, begin it; boldness has genius, power and magic in it". In modern parlance this means *just do it!*

The more often you ride your hunches, the more confidence you will gain in doing so. And the more you'll come to trust you live in a benevolent universe, which has your best interest at heart. What constitutes your calling will not be the same for your mother, your brother, your best friend, or your teacher, so there is little point in heeding their well-intended advice if it doesn't resonate with you. Only you can know (by doing it) what is right for you so don't be afraid to experiment when you have the inkling to do so. "Rivers and roads lead people on," said artist Georgia O'Keeffe.

In awakening your intuitive vision the greater challenge will always be to get out of – and stay out of – your own way long enough to allow your innate ingenuity free range. Be excited and curious about the images that rise up like atolls out of the ocean and abide by them when they seem to nudge you in a particular direction. There is a divine moment when it comes to the materialisation of a vision when providence is ready to move too. In the interim it pays to cultivate patience, which is something I had to learn. But please, please find the courage to do something with the guidance you receive, otherwise it's like uncovering treasure and throwing it away.

Applications

We have seen how making the Intuitive Vision Board is particularly useful in gaining clarity when you are facing challenges or transitioning through change. This process can support young people and students too by helping them to make wise decisions at the different choice points in their academic career. It can also help you cope with adversity and find a route through a crisis by articulating a route that you cannot yet see.

Here are some common applications of the Intuitive Vision Board I have employed. You may well think of others besides. If you'd like to talk to me about providing any of these workshops please enquire at www.marynonde.com/contact/.

Friendship or peer groups

Gather a group of friends or peers and share the creative space together. Everyone makes an individual vision board and each takes a moment at the end to communicate the highlights to the group. This is a lovely occasion to get to know one another better and to forge the bond between you. Another time you might consider making a communal vision board that holds the values of the group and your aspirations for being together. It's easy enough to obtain duplicates afterwards so everyone has a copy.

Family

This is a shared experience in which you create the Intuitive Vision Board together. It's a way to ensure everyone's needs are being expressed and heard by all family members. It's also useful for rallying the family together around a common cause by creating a joint vision for the future, a bond of love and a sense of belonging. This exercise is not about creating synthesis or aiming for a convergence of ideas, although this may happen. It's more about making sure the idiosyncrasies of each individual are voiced and accommodated so that the whole is strengthened by this. The finished product can be displayed where the family come together – to eat or to share a desk space perhaps.

Before progressing to the collective board, each family member might prefer to make their own Intuitive Vision Board first, even if it's a smaller size. This allows them to become familiar with the process and gain confidence with the tool before making their contribution to the family board.

Occasionally I have run three-generational Intuitive Vision Board workshops and it's delightful to see the different approaches and perspectives on life each generation contributes. You might like to include the grandparents when you are making your individual or communal vision boards together.

Couples and partners

Making an Intuitive Vision Board together is a beautiful way to ensure individual needs are honoured and accommodated in the relationship while providing a focus for the life you want to co-create together. You might each prefer to create an individual vision board first on an earlier occasion, before progressing to the couple's board you will make together.

01: Initiation

02: Invocation

03: Invention

04: Inception

05: Immersion

06: Illumination

07: Integration

08: Inauguration

01: Initiation

02: Invocation

03: Invention

04: Inception

05: Immersion

06: Illumination

07: Integration

08: Inauguration

It's always a good idea at the end of the creative session to allow plenty of time for you both to share your boards and to hear what the other has to say in response to this. The Intuitive Vision Board is an excellent communication tool.

Corporates and organisations

The Intuitive Vision Board workshop works very well as a team-awayday, a leadership development tool, and as a bonding exercise. Not only does it empower the individual to be more creative and to contribute ideas outside the box, which is top of the agenda for many organisations, but it also encourages engagement with other team members as they get to know one another as people beyond the roles and responsibilities of their job.

I worked with a global company where budget restrictions only permitted team leaders to gather in person once or twice a year. In the meantime they needed to work together remotely and communicate best practice. On this occasion before Christmas we'd demarcated half a day for the Intuitive Vision Board workshop. The process naturally encourages openness so there is no need for anyone to be guarded or modify their vision to fit in with the group.

When it came to presenting their vision board, each person was informed that they need only share as much as they felt comfortable doing. As it was, the workshop went down a storm and everyone was energised by it, so nobody felt a need to hold back on sharing.

I'd like to end this chapter with a fascinating story about the benefits of making a family vision board together, as seen through the eyes of the mother and wife who encouraged the family to do it.

How the world opened its doors

Morgan was in a time of personal transition and flux, which was playing out in her family life too. It was time for her once again to stop and re-evaluate. Rather than make a vision board on her own and drag the family along with the content afterwards as she had historically done, she wanted them all to play a part in creating the next chapter of the life they hoped to share together. So I took the

115

01: Initiation

02: Invocation

03: Invention

04: Inception

05: Immersion

06: Illumination

07: Integration

08: Inauguration

Intuitive Vision Board workshop on tour to their home and this is what transpired though Morgan's eyes.

"My first vision board with Mary was a personal prophecy about returning to my feminine self: switching off the corporate superwoman who had created a very successful business and switching on the yogi, the vegan, the healer. I was desperate to shed the bread-winning, decision-making mantle and become a woman ready to receive. It was not an easy transition; it took time and there were moments when I felt very lost. Besides we were in a difficult place as a couple after 24 years together, while my relationship with my sister was challenging too. Losing both parents within six months of one another in very painful circumstances had left me in a vulnerable place. It was altogether a heart-rending time.

"The idea of making a vision board together initially met with resistance from both my son (age 12) and my husband. But I persevered because I believed it was important for us. I had no idea what would come from it but I trusted Mary to create a safe space and her gentle shepherding through the process would give us what we needed to express our innermost desires. Surprisingly, my husband who'd been very reluctant at first, became totally immersed in the process and took great pains to place his images intricately into the whole. He also took on the self-appointed role of policing our activity to ensure we each had equal opportunity to be heard.

"Creating the vision board together was no effort at all: no friction, no dispute. I can't say at all who put what on where; it just happened. What was extraordinary to me was that with three of us choosing the images independently – and in silence – a consistent three-part theme emerged between us: the desire for closeness, family time together, and to travel in the big outdoors.

"In the early weeks, after creating our family road map, I'd look at our board and think nothing's happening! But then I reminded myself that six months elapsed before I saw any action on my personal vision board. The first sign of life was when I found a yoga practitioner in the US I liked and connected up with her online. She'd just returned from South America with a beautiful stripy rug just like the one on our family board. We're moving in the right direction, I felt.

"I'd been very privileged to be in travel marketing for 30 years, yet we'd done very little travel of late since I was no longer bringing in a regular corporate salary. We had no plans ahead and nothing in the diary, yet all over our vision board there were inspiring worldwide destinations we had all chosen. I'd just received my first travel writing commission when we made the family board, and that was for a short-haul solo trip.

"But after six months living with the board everything changed. In the following year the opportunities to write and to travel came thick and fast. Below are just some of the places I visited with my family – *all* of which appeared on the vision board accompanied by specific features. For example: a sunken fire pit, an elephant sanctuary, a couple canoeing, riding and swimming with horses. It was mind-blowing – and it didn't escape the notice of either my son or my husband:

» Waterberg region of South Africa (all three of us).

» Mauritius (my husband and I) – 10 days together including our 25th wedding anniversary and the opportunity to revisit a place we'd been to 20 years previously.

» Sri Lanka and The Maldives (son and sister) – a very precious time. My sister got to know my son properly for the first time. And, as we chatted, we healed some old wounds.

» Ibiza (with my best friend and Samuel's godmother) – pure fun.

» Italy skiing (with my son) – I'm not an accomplished skier but enjoyed sharing this precious time with him and his school friends.

» Venice school trip (all three) – to hear my son open the mass at St Mark's Basilica is something my mother would have been amazed by.

"In hindsight what started out as a beautiful pictorial vision of places and experiences we aspired to, I can honestly say we did most of them within 18 months. My love of travel – or should I say our love of travel – was well and truly reignited and shared. As if that wasn't enough, one of the travel articles I wrote got picked up by a TV broadcaster who approached me to set up a new travel programme. The monthly programme will run across a network of 27 stations in the UK and reach 6.4 million adults a month. Not only did creating our vision board together reunite and inspire us as a family, I hope it will now inspire millions of other people to visit places they may never have dreamed possible. All because we committed to spending the afternoon together and were willing to listen to what our hearts desired."

In Chapter 8 – Inauguration – you are on the final leg of the creative journey, in which we explore how the Intuitive Vision Board can enable you to become a visionary in your own lifetime.

01: Initiation

02: Invocation

03: Invention

04: Inception

05: Immersion

06: Illumination

07: Integration

08: Inauguration

01: Initiation

02: Invocation

03: Invention

04: Inception

05: Immersion

06: Illumination

07: Integration

08: Inauguration

"Two roads diverged in a yellow wood... and I – I took the one less travelled by and that has made all the difference."

Robert Frost, Poet

01: Initiation

02: Invocation

03: Invention

04: Inception

05: Immersion

06: Illumination

07: Integration

08: Inauguration

Chapter 8

INAUGURATION

On becoming a visionary

Have you ever known something extraordinary happen that changed the course of your life forever? This happened to me when I was 38 years old. Long before I'd invented my Intuitive Vision Board process I received a vision – a prophetic, show-stopping vision. A bit like Moses and the burning bush on the mountainside, except I was in a conference room in London at the time. This visitation arrived completely unannounced and knocked me out. When I came around, I was on the floor and the words *Dancing for Joy* were on my lips. Over the years since, a chain of events has unfolded, which has had enormous consequences for my life, none of which I'd thought of or planned for before the vision I'd received in London.

At the time of the vision I'd just completed a sea change in career in which I'd sold my share of a marketing consultancy and retrained in Feng Shui in Seattle. My teacher, Denise Linn, was visiting London for the Mind Body Spirit Fair to deliver a seminar on cellular regeneration and she invited me to be on her team. We're in a room full of people (about 150 of them) and I'm standing at the edge of the room to frame the healing space for the visitors, along with six other colleagues. My eyes are closed and I am leaning back against the wall, totally relaxed and in a meditative state. Denise is leading the guided meditation, accompanied by the heartbeat rhythm on her Native American drum. At the height of the meditation, with the drumming at its most intense, she utters the immortal words: "You are now back, now back to Source ..." at which point I pass out.

Seconds earlier, I'd watched a fireball of energy hurtle towards me in my mind's eye and hit me in the hara centre. As the energy rose up inside me I felt nauseous and fainted. As I came around, the first thing I noticed were my stockinged legs stretched out in front of me. When I realised I was prostrate on the floor and visitors were coming to my aid, I was embarrassed too, since I was there to support them, not for them to support me.

I was neither tired nor hungry, neither before nor after the incident. On my feet again, I was totally bemused by the experience. When we came together as a team afterwards all ears were keen to hear what had transpired. What could I say? I'd never fainted before – or since. Still shocked by the experience, I could only report the words on my lips: *Dancing for Joy*. What they meant I had no idea.

121

01: Initiation

02: Invocation

03: Invention

04: Inception

05: Immersion

06: Illumination

07: Integration

08: Inauguration

Download

Two days later I was at home listening to Native American drumming, when I received the complete vision for *Dancing for Joy* in a single transmission. It was quite complex, so I hastily wrote it down. Because it entailed the creation of a large meeting space and a retreat centre, I paid for an architect to produce drawings of my ideas.

If you'd asked me had I any inkling about this vision before it happened the answer would have been no. I'd never entertained the idea of creating a retreat centre before.

If you'd asked me on the day of Denise's seminar had I felt out of sorts, the answer again would have been no. I was on form and simply there to help.

Did the vision significantly change what I did with my life from that time forward? The answer was a definite yes, although I didn't know it would at the time. I barely knew what a vision was. In my corporate days, I was more accustomed to think in terms of a mission statement, setting goals and then creating a strategy to fulfil both.

Destiny

The week following the London experience, my French boyfriend and I were due to hike the Grand Canyon from the North Rim to the south. This trip had been planned 12 months before because accommodation at the bottom of the canyon, in Phantom Ranch, was at a premium. Only days before we were due to fly, we received notification that storms had washed the North Rim trail away and this meant we couldn't walk it.

We adjusted our plans and flew to Las Vegas instead and viewed the Grand Canyon by helicopter, planning to walk the South Rim a few days later. Staying at the Aria Resort, I asked if they could recommend a massage therapist and was introduced to Richard.

Now I'm 20 floors up in Richard's apartment overlooking the bright lights of Vegas while Richard orchestrates a most extraordinary body therapy session. This wasn't massage as I knew it, yet with the help of his assistant and my boyfriend, my limbs and torso were folded and stretched in every conceivable way to music. It must have released something in my body because the following day I conceived, which I only discovered to my surprise on my return to England. Like *Dancing for Joy*, the pregnancy wasn't planned either. Now what was I to do with *Dancing for Joy* with a child on the way?

01: Initiation

02: Invocation

03: Invention

04: Inception

05: Immersion

06: Illumination

07: Integration

08: Inauguration

Wake-up calls

Twelve months passed in a nanosecond as I embraced motherhood with fervour. I barely gave a second thought to *Dancing for Joy*. Then, almost a year to the date from when I'd received the vision, things started to happen. The first time I was stationary in my car, with my daughter strapped into the baby carrier beside me. As if from nowhere a car reversed into the side of us. Fortunately, neither of us were injured but there was about £2,000 worth of damage and my car disappeared for two weeks to be fixed.

A further 12 months passed and my daughter was by now a toddler, when a similar incident occurred with her strapped into the car seat. We were approaching a roundabout, when the car behind me hadn't noticed I'd stopped and went into the back of me. Fortunately again we were not injured although my car received another £2,000 worth of damage.

Yet another year passes and I am now regularly teaching Feng Shui and conducting consultations in homes and in organisations. *Dancing for Joy* lurks in the recesses of my mind and I occasionally ponder how I might move it forward. One day, I'm reversing out of a car parking space, when a car turns into the back me. You've guessed it! Another £2,000 worth of damage and no car for two weeks. This time my husband is furious and I am dumbfounded.

Perhaps it was a little overdue but I decided to sit still and meditate on the matter. Even though I'd given *Dancing for Joy* a lower priority, clearly the idea was stubborn and not about to let me off the hook so easily. I felt nudged to do something with it since on each occasion I was stationary behind the wheel of my car, which was a suitable metaphor I thought. And with my daughter sat beside me each time she seemed to be implicated as an accomplice. Then it dawned on me that nothing could happen unless my now-husband was able to step up to the mark and I could relinquish the role of major breadwinner. Within a week of getting this clarity, I fell pregnant again...

To be or not to be

Once more I pushed *Dancing for Joy* to one side. Once more I avoided a confrontation with my husband and concentrated on my work, the toddler and the pregnancy. However, my body reserves were low from juggling it all. I was by then 43 years old, and I miscarried at three months. With a heavy heart, knowing this was probably my last chance for another child, I didn't recover physically either and was unable to work. My savings were quickly eaten into because my husband didn't have any savings and his salary did not cover our overheads. This time I insisted he take whatever work he could to allow me time to recover. His response to the gauntlet was to return to France. Sadly a divorce ensued.

123

01: Initiation

02: Invocation

03: Invention

04: Inception

05: Immersion

06: Illumination

07: Integration

08: Inauguration

What about the *Dancing for Joy* vision? I am a single parent now with the sole financial and parental responsibility for my four-year-old. To my credit, I did manage to outline a business plan and visit some suitable venues that might lend themselves to becoming the centre. But without money and support, the odds were against me and I felt the *Dancing for Joy* vision, as originally conceived, slipping through my fingers like quicksilver… and so I let go. I determined if I couldn't physically create the *Dancing for Joy* centre, I would become it instead.

What have all these weird and wonderful visionary happenings back then got to do with the Intuitive Vision Boards today? I had no idea either where it was all leading. It was only when I came to write this book that I spotted the connection, the golden thread that had been weaving its way through my life for the past 23 years. I was astounded.

Follow your bliss

All I knew at the time was that I was stuck. I'd gained a vision but I'd lost a baby and a husband. However, I'm a great believer in *following your bliss*, a philosophy expounded by Joseph Campbell, who I'd first come across while studying anthropology. I believe that when you've lost your way, following your bliss – that which makes your heart sing – will always, eventually, help to get you back on track. One of my early joys was to dance.

And so it was that I started to dance again, regularly (remember the role of the hobby I mentioned in Chapter 7?). By the time my daughter turned seven, the age I'd taken up dancing as a child, I returned to university to do a PGCE in Dance. I became fascinated with the therapeutic and healing aspect of dance-movement, and this interest evolved into an MA in Somatic Arts Psychotherapy. I began hiring village halls to deliver my first classes and workshops. I incorporated expressive arts into my classes. Can you see how it was only a question of time before I would be running my first Intuitive Vision Board workshop?

The gift

Towards the end of the MA studies my auntie died. She had taken care of me since birth when my mother couldn't on account of a chronic illness. Now my auntie was about to help me again by leaving me a small inheritance. Before I'd loaned most of this to a friend on the promise that it would be repaid (which sadly never happened), I went to Marin County, California to work with dance pioneer Anna Halprin. For one luxurious week, I joined other students in her large indoor studio and outdoors on her dance platform among the redwood trees, which was a dancers' space to die for.

One day after training I took a drive in my hire car, following my nose, and heading in the direction of the Pacific Ocean. I espied an impressive sign by the roadside: "Spirit Rock". I swung into the long and meandering driveway that curved gently upwards towards a magnificent timber-framed building on top of the hill. It was a meditation and retreat centre. The main workshop space was vast and constructed from wood in the shape of an octagon, which is considered to be a very auspicious shape in Feng Shui. It had floor-to-ceiling glass windows and an apex roof.

And the biggest surprise of all? *It was almost the replica of the site and building I had visualised as Dancing for Joy 14 years earlier.* It took my breath away!

When I enquired at reception about the history of Spirit Rock, I learnt that the design and build had been created roughly the same time I received the vision in England – only this centre was the brainchild of Jack Kornfield. Jack is one of the world's leading teachers of Buddhist mindfulness. Presumably he'd not only received his vision around the same time as me but also had the wherewithal to build it. And where else in the world had this idea landed, I wondered?

Multiple discoveries

Elizabeth Gilbert talks about an idea as a bundle of unmanifest energy looking for a good nest to settle in, in her book *Big Magic*. She also refers to "multiple discoveries", which was first recognised by the scientific world. It would appear that the same idea can land in the nest of several potential incubators simultaneously, on the basis that at least one of them will manage to sit on the egg long enough to hatch it, my metaphor for it. The process is not as random as it first sounds. Unmanifest energy is infinitely intelligent and only seeks out ideal suitors. Despite not having run a centre before, I had created a successful business and I clearly had the passion for what should take place there. I'd even shown willing to have a go in challenging circumstances. But I hadn't been able to pull this particular vision off whereas Jack Kornfield had.

I wrote to Jack and shared the synchronicity but I didn't receive an answer. I imagined he had more important things to do and might have found my story a little far-fetched. If I hadn't written the vision down, crafted a business plan and drafted architect's drawings, I might have begun to wonder about it myself.

125

01: Initiation
02: Invocation
03: Invention
04: Inception
05: Immersion
06: Illumination
07: Integration
08: Inauguration

"Who looks outside dreams; who looks inside awakes"
– Carl Jung

Now here I am writing all this down in 2018, some 23 years later.

It won't surprise you to know that since the original visionary *Dancing for Joy* transmission, my interest in visions and visioning was awakened and captivated. Although I didn't consciously set out with this in mind, it later transpired that my MA was to add considerable weight to my understanding of how visions and visioning could occur. By now I'd studied Carl Jung, who spurred on a generation of bestselling authors who I'd also read in the fields of psychology, psychotherapy and mythology, including Joseph Campbell. Jung's particular genius was to introduce spirituality into psychology and metaphysical thought. His fascination with spiritual phenomena cost him his mentor and friendship with Sigmund Freud, who wasn't having any of it. But Jung stayed true to his particular calling and we wouldn't be where we are today if he hadn't.

It's to Jung we can attribute concepts which are now so commonplace in coaching and counselling circles, such as archetypes (images, patterns and symbols), synchronicity, and the shadow self. Jung also raised the profile of intuition, creativity, and our feeling nature to give them equal credence alongside rational thinking and sensation to broaden our understanding of people. This knowledge has infiltrated the corporate world and is the basis for several talent profiling tools we take for granted.

"That which stands in the way is the way" – Marcus Aurelius

From Jung I also learned about the collective unconscious, which I have mentioned in earlier chapters. Surprise, surprise, this is the land where unmanifest ideas and intuitive visions come from. Jung himself frequently experienced lucid dreams and prophetic visions. Experimenting with his own psychic material, he established a way to receive this information from the collective unconscious by engaging the active imagination through creativity, authentic movement, the somatic arts and psychotherapeutic process.

And so it came to pass the MA degree in Somatic Art Psychotherapy that I studied helped me to migrate *Dancing for Joy* in the literal sense of the vision into the Intuitive Vision Board – the creative process with which I could facilitate the visions of others.

The Intuitive Vision Board has become my primary tool of choice in helping people vision what wonderful possibilities there are in store for them beyond the usual end-gaming decision-making of the egoic mind. It's an emergent visioning process with depth and pedigree. It stands alone among other vision board methods in drawing exclusively on the intuition and imagination to dialogue with the collective unconscious. It provides a foolproof way to break out of Logical-Left thinking and permit innovative pathways to open up naturally.

The more important question posed by this process is not *what do you want in your life?* but rather *what life wants to be created through you?*

Inclusive

In designing the workshop, I had also intuitively replicated the best conditions in which visions and spiritual guidance can be received by the ordinary person in a more user-friendly way. I realised Moses' burning bush experience or passing out on the floor would not be everybody's idea of fun.

The Intuitive Vision Board is a readily accessible tool that can be used by people of all ages, nationalities and genders. Both individuals and organisations can receive a vision to empower and enrich their lives, including those who don't consider themselves to have a creative bone in their body and feel they were born disconnected from their right brain. You don't need to be artistically endowed or mystically predisposed to make the Intuitive Vision Board. Nor does it require you to learn a special set of skills, although, as we've seen, it does require special preparation beforehand for you to be receptive.

"Life is the dancer and you are the dance" – Eckhart Tolle

My visionary formula was also influenced by the spiritual teachings of Eckhart Tolle, who published *The Power of Now*, shortly before I embarked on the MA degree. Consequently, I go to great lengths to ensure a person is fully present in their whole body before they constellate their vision, in much the way I was when I received *Dancing for Joy*. I figured Tolle's reference to primordial intelligence is synonymous with the unfathomable dimension Jung called the collective unconscious. Tolle also maintains most desires are conjured up by the ego and motivated by its unquenchable desire to manifest countless stuff believing it will make us happy. Hedonistic I'd call it.

Organic growth

Since that original visionary incident in London, my life has evolved more organically and with less interference on my part, which is the opposite to how I conducted myself in the early part of my career. I am now comfortable knowing there are invisible hands

127

01: Initiation

02: Invocation

03: Invention

04: Inception

05: Immersion

06: Illumination

07: Integration

08: Inauguration

steering the wheel of life. I have come to trust in their benevolent intentions, not just for my personal benefit but in how they have directed me towards making the best contribution I can to the whole.

I grew into this perspective and it was not without resistance at the outset. Over the years of making the Intuitive Vision Board, I have increasingly learned to let go when it comes to the creative act and to allow the irrational nature of intuition to lead me down roads less travelled. I have found them to be far more interesting and rewarding than anything I could have planned myself. This work has become my vocation, as I have specialised in encouraging ordinary people to create extraordinary lives and become visionaries in their own lifetimes. My Feng Shui practice sits beautifully alongside this in preparing the home and office for the vision to take root and flourish in a conducive environment, without there being obstacles to undermine it.

I've yet to enjoy a similar salary to that which I took home as the joint owner of a marketing consultancy with Fortune 500 clients. However, I am proud to have raised my daughter on my own. And I did need to start all over again financially, age 56, so I haven't done too badly so far. Most importantly, I am now firmly aligned with my life purpose and this is deeply meaningful to me. If I got down to my last penny – and you can see I've come close to this at times – I would not trade my soul for the satisfaction I've gained in helping midwife the visions of others and encouraging them to lead their most authentic lives.

I've created this timeline to show you how my story holds together, charting as it does my experience with visions and visioning over 24 years, as described in this book.

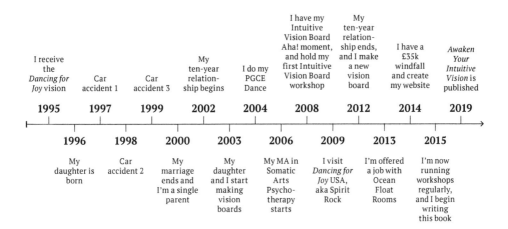

7 golden rules for visionaries

In conclusion, here are the seven golden rules for awakening your intuitive vision to become a visionary in your own lifetime.

1. Maintain the connection

Stay connected to your vision because if you leave it too long without doing anything with it, the opportunities move on. The Intuitive Vision Board can aid you in this, acting as an anchor and a familiar landmark to which you can return over and over again, when the outer distractions of life might cause you to lose the plot. The Intuitive Vision Board can be your muse to provide hope, reassurance and guidance so you don't have to rely on friends, family, partner or your coach, especially when they may not always be available – or affordable.

2. Stop watching the clock

Visions live in a time-zone of their own beyond clock time. Even though the vision may be crystal clear from the outset, the right moment for it to come to fruition is probably not immediate and may be many months, if not years, hence. The Intuitive Vision Board acts like a beacon, magnetising you towards the materialisation of its content and prompting you to take action in line with its purpose, even when you are not consciously aware of doing so.

Meanwhile, you must be patient and not attempt to speed things up or force matters along – by adding another image to your vision board because Logical-Left has told you to, for example. Living with the uncertainty, wondering if anything is actually happening below the surface of life, is the most uncomfortable part of the visionary's journey – but it's what needs to happen. So hands off!

3. Illogical by nature

The Intuitive Vision Board not only conveys the "what?" but also the "how?" of what wants to be created. The manner in which the images coexist and their relationship to one another can provide vital clues. But give up trying to comprehend this just by staring at your newly-created board. Allow yourself to absorb the whole without thinking too long and hard about it. Let it wash over you.

Universal energy, which is infinite and pure, wants to flow through each of us. It has communicated with you through the Intuitive Vision Board. This formless intelligence can make non-sequential connections between what might appear to Logical-Left to be quite random events. At a later time you may return to your board to join up the dots with a knowing grin on your face.

4. Embrace it all

There are many and various steps to be undertaken between where your Intuitive Vision Board begins and where it will end. These steps can appear nonsensical, yet if they are on your board and you are drawn to pursue them please do so, even while Logical-Left is ranting in your other ear that this is a complete detour. Sometimes these steps are necessary to clear out psychological or physiological obstacles that are blocking your path and restricting your progress. Staying wise to these prompts and finding the courage and determination to act on them is essential to the visionary.

You are embarking on a transformational journey and you must be prepared to change and grow along the way. The trick is to engage willingly with *whatever* presents itself, even when it's messy and appears to be an irritating inconvenience – or a disaster even. And remember to celebrate every milestone reached without becoming too fixated on its purpose, the necessity of which will become apparent in good time.

5. Metaphorical not literal

For several years I pursued *Dancing for Joy* literally – to create a meeting venue and retreat centre. There was value in doing so because I visited some lovely places and it had me expand my outlook beyond the limitations of the single-parent box. Then it dawned on me there was perhaps another way to work with the vision once the literal interpretation of it seemed to run out of steam.

It will be the same for you. The words and imagery on your Intuitive Vision Board are more poetic, symbolic and numinous by nature as opposed to literal. This means the metaphorical content of your vision will need unravelling once the dream is over but only insofar as it's possible to unlock something of a mystical nature. Sometimes, the final comprehension only occurs long after the vision – or elements of it – have manifested.

01: Initiation

02: Invocation

03: Invention

04: Inception

05: Immersion

06: Illumination

07: Integration

08: Inauguration

And just because you are now the proud owner of the Intuitive Vision Board, this is no guarantee it will be plain sailing to develop it. Or you will live happily ever after. Best not to expect either of these and then be pleasantly surprised. What you can know for sure is you will live wisely and your life will be enriched and expansive when driven by your vision and your calling. And when things get a little ropey, why not try this technique I use to calm myself by saying: "Look at what *even* the Dalai Lama had to go through, Mary!"

6. Do it anyway

If your vision appears beyond your current capabilities, you can nevertheless trust you have the predisposition for it and the resources you need will somehow miraculously appear as you move towards it – or morph into something related as they did in my case. Your task is to follow the flow of your creative energy and at a pace that doesn't compromise your well-being. This is supposed to be a spiritual collaboration with primordial intelligence, not a takeover by it. The best you can do is allow it to happen and try not to second guess what is required of you.

You are advised to stay clear of – or keep quiet around – those who may want to put the stops on you because what you are doing doesn't make sense to them or they are disconcerted by it. Sometimes friends and family would prefer us to stay the way we are, not for our sakes but for theirs. Most people don't like change and would prefer you not to upset their equilibrium by growing bigger than your boots. This attitude arises from fear not love and you must still do what you are called to do anyway.

7. Tiny vision, big impact

A vision doesn't have to be massive to count. Your willingness to receive whatever guidance attends you on your Intuitive Vision Board, to inspire your year ahead, is good enough justification to become a visionary in your own lifetime. Ideas, as we have seen, are always on the lookout for a good champion to execute them. It's also the case that even when you are predisposed to the vision, the eggs won't hatch unless you receive the right support to do so. This may call for a radical upheaval as it did in both cases for me. Some of these changes I accepted willingly and other times I had to be pulled along by my hair. But ultimately it was all for my own good and the greater good of my calling.

Life is a challenge and there are many hurdles to surmount along the way. However, by awakening your intuition, by embracing your vision as laid down for you on the Intuitive Vision Board, and growing down into your sacred assignment – whatever form it takes

01: Initiation

02: Invocation

03: Invention

04: Inception

05: Immersion

06: Illumination

07: Integration

08: Inauguration

– you'll embrace more opportunities than you ever entertained were possible. And when the outer circumstances of your life feel a bit uncertain, your Intuitive Vision Board is the place to return to be reminded of the unique potential waiting to be cultivated by you. As an act of service to the world you and your vision will make a significant difference, while you will get to lead a rich, authentic and meaningful life yourself.

Mary Nondé

"Awaken Your Intuitive Vision – creating possibilities you never knew existed"

www.marynonde.com

FURTHER READING

Ted Andrews, *Animal Speak: The Spiritual & Magical Powers of Creatures Great and Small*

Angeles Arrien, *Signs of Life – The Five Universal Shapes and How to Use Them*

Viktor Frankl, *Man's Search for Meaning*

Elizabeth Gilbert, *Big Magic: Creative Living Beyond Fear*

Caroline Myss, *Anatomy of the Spirit: The Seven Stages of Power and Healing*

Ken Robinson, https://www.ted.com/speakers/sir_ken_robinson

Mel Schwartz, *The Possibility Principle*

Louisa Thomsen Brits, *The Book of Hygge: The Danish Art of Living Well*

Eckhart Tolle, *A New Earth*

Eckhart Tolle, *The Power of Now: A Guide to Spiritual Enlightenment*

GLOSSARY OF TERMS

Active imagination is a method of communication which bridges the gap between the conscious (thought) and the unconscious mind (dreams, fantasies, visions) through creative self-expression, giving voice to ideas not normally entertained.

Alpha brain waves occur when your brain is idling such as when you're daydreaming, practising mindfulness or engaged in meditation. Alpha waves can also be generated by aerobic type of exercise like running, walking or dancing.

Aura is the distinctive, invisible energy field surrounding a person, thing or place, which is an essential part of them and the combined result of mental, emotional and spiritual activity.

Beta brain waves are the fastest moving and reflect the state of mind you are in when problem-solving, brainstorming or studying. Over-usage without sufficient downtime can result in burn-out.

Calling, aka as your vocation, refers to a strong inner impulse to a particular course of action that may defy logic but puts your talents and capabilities to good effect, especially with conviction of a divine influence.

Convergent thinking refers to the thought processing ability that can sift through many available options to arrive at the 'correct' answer, particularly to standard questions that do not require significant creativity.

Constellate means to group or cluster together, with each component in the right relationship and at the right distance from the others, such as stars in a constellation.

Daimon is the Ancient Greek spelling of the Latin word "daemon". Both refer to a god, godlike, spiritual power or muse that guides and protects an individual, to support you in attaining your highest levels of achievement and happiness.

Delta brain waves are the slowest moving and occur primarily during our deepest state of dreamless sleep, which is so essential for healing and regeneration.

Divergent thinking is the thought processing method used to generate creative ideas around a given problem by exploring many possible solutions in a free-flowing, non-linear manner.

Emergent thinking®, defined by Mel Schwartz, applies the scientific concept of emergence to thought processing in which both the starting point and the end destination are not defined in advance. The field of possibility emerges and unfolds as you engage with it, as when creating a vision on an Intuitive Vision Board.

Eudaimonic is the drive towards the attainment of long-term happiness and self-actualisation by discovering your place in the world.

Gestalt is a highly intelligent organised field of information with specific properties that belong together and the whole is greater than the sum of its parts.

Hedonic/Hedonistic is the drive towards short-term happiness and based on the notion that increased pleasure-seeking and decreased pain leads to maximum fulfilment.

Logical-Left describes the activity of the left-hand side of the brain associated with linear, analytical, rational, methodical thinking.

Manifestation is when something of an unformed nature becomes real and concrete, based on the ancient life principle that if we visualise what we want, we will attract it to us.

Remarkable-Right describes the activity of the right-hand side of the brain associated with non-linear thinking, creativity, intuition and the imagination.

Source refers to a place, person or thing from which something originates or can be obtained in the spiritual sense of the word, otherwise interchangeable with the words "god", "the divine", and the "universe".

Theta brain waves occur during sleep and are also observed in deeper states of meditation and during active imagination. The language of Theta is dreamlike, metaphorical and non-descript.

Undermind is another way of describing the intelligent and under-utilised unconscious or sixth sense which affords us the ability to register events and make extraordinary connections in ways that defy logic and are almost magical.

ABOUT
MARY NONDÉ

Author, Teacher, Intuitive Coach
and Lifelong Visionary

Author of
AWAKEN YOUR INTUITIVE VISION
Unlocking possibilities you never knew existed

Mary Nondé is based in Bourne End, Buckinghamshire, UK on the River Thames.

To find out more about Mary, continue reading below.

To attend an Intuitive Vision Board workshop write to
www.marynonde.com/contact/

To enquire about receiving an Intuitive Vision Board workshop on your turf write to
www.marynonde.com/contact/

My calling

I believe in the power of the intuition, the imagination and creativity to unlock the hidden gifts in people and organisations. The tools I use to access this diamond mine of latent potential are the Intuitive Vision Board with Empowerment Coaching, Feng Shui practice and Movement-Art therapy.

Culture of things

My adult life began with me studying Anthropology at Durham University, considered a trifle unusual at the time. Durham, in the cooler north of England, was a far cry from the mild shores of South Devon where I grew up by the sea. I still remember the fur coat from Oxfam purchased in an attempt to stay warm.

As anthropologists, we were taught to pay close attention to people's behaviour because this is where we found evidence of a value system. Words can quickly become post-rationalisations and can too easily be misconstrued by the listener. Actions are what shape a person, a society and a culture. To this day I subscribe to this perspective: it's not what you say, it's what you do that counts.

Intuitive

After my degree, I gravitated towards marketing in a field that has since been superseded by online shopping – mail order book clubs. I cut my teeth here, before launching a direct marketing consultancy with my business partner. Over eight years the consultancy grew into a successful business, dealing with mostly Fortune 500 companies.

With my anthropological filter always uppermost, I naturally tuned into the unspoken ground rules, driving an individual or organisation. The not-so-obvious held the juice and has always fascinated me, which is why I'm intuitively drawn to it.

Return on investment

In our own agency, we had a team of 15 and beautiful offices, which we'd created so clients could enjoy some respite away from London. For them Bracknell was rural.

Staff were a mystery to me. We had good talent and invested regularly in skills and personal development. We paid good salaries. But I felt the business only enjoyed the tip of the iceberg in terms of what the individuals were capable of delivering to the organisation. I couldn't find a way to liberate them from their assigned roles and uncover more potential – despite talent profiling – and it troubled me.

When I gave up the consultancy to become a mother, this conundrum went with me. It wasn't until I returned to university that I inadvertently stumbled upon the answers I was looking for. This solution I'm now able to share with clients to unlock the latent potential in themselves and their companies.

Living mindfully

My flair for sensing the not-so-obvious gave me additional insights when it came to the arrangement of living and working spaces. I trained in Feng Shui, mostly with Denise Linn in Seattle, and I have remained passionate about the art and science of living mindfully and arranging space to support the vision.

Still with my anthropological filter, I see my role with Feng Shui is to make people aware of the culture of their homes and offices through the imprint they leave on their environment. When this is out of kilter with their desired business or personal outcomes, I show them how to fix it. I teach. I consult. And I have travelled, mostly in the UK, France and the USA.

In the early days, I did many consultations with my baby in a sling. When she was older, she gravitated towards dolls houses – four in total. I imagine Feng Shui must have rubbed off on her too because she spent many hours creating lovely homes for Sylvanian animals.

Dancing queen

Four years as a parent and I am on my own. My instinct was to bring the scene of operations closer to home and manage my portfolio – as a mother, homemaker, entrepreneur – under one roof. To simplify life I was persuaded to buy a puppy – and it was the best decision I ever made!

To stay sane, I started dancing again, which I'd begun age four as a ballerina in a pink tutu and developed into a tap-dancing impresario. I obtained a PGCE in Dance and began teaching creative dance to children and organic movement to adults. Meanwhile my studies evolved into a Master's Degree in Somatic Art Psychotherapy at the University of Chichester.

Towards the end of my student life I received the inspiration for the Intuitive Vision Board workshop. Here was the tool I'd been looking for to unlock the latent potential in people. When we connect to the core of our creativity, we source our real power and become our most authentic – and that's to be celebrated.

I've since delivered the Intuitive Vision Board workshop to over a thousand men, women and children from all walks of life.

My mentors

I have a daily practice in the somatic arts. My home and work space is always Feng Shui-friendly. And I make a new Intuitive Vision Board every year. I have been fortunate to have had some wonderful teachers, notably Denise Linn, Helen Poynor, Miranda Tuffnell, Claude Coldy and Anna Halprin.

Sadly Dr Jill Hayes, who was such an inspiration as my university tutor, has passed away. Jill used to say: "What I respect about you the most, Mary, is your capacity to stay true to your creative calling no matter the outer circumstances of your life." It touches me greatly to recall her words, because I didn't understand what she meant at the time. Many of us long to be seen for who we truly are and I was seen and acknowledged by Jill.

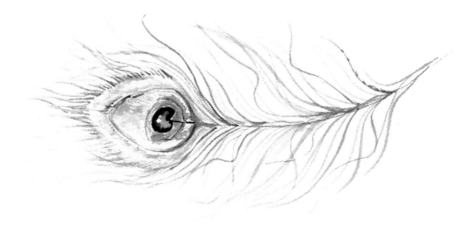

REVIEWS FOR AWAKEN YOUR INTUITIVE VISION

"Mary's story-telling ability is second to none. Her book is engaging, funny, quirky, educational and warm. She describes with clarity how to reach, and surface, our unconscious thoughts to remind ourselves of who we are and what our deepest hopes are. Mary entwines tales of her own life and the experiences of her clients who have created an Intuitive Vision Board to illustrate the power of our unconscious minds and how, when we allow it to speak, we find direction and purpose again, in surprising ways. The book explains step by step how to create your own Intuitive Vision Board and provides guidance on how to begin to interpret your creation. Its real power is in enabling us to be curious again about our own future and feel positive about the possibilities that lie before us."

Lindsey Wheeler,
CEO, www.safireconsulting.co.uk

"A delicious read which I pretty much gobbled up in one sitting. I found the book to be a true and thorough account of the visioning process I experienced with Mary. And, having read the book, I now understand more about why it was so powerful. Those parts of me I'd been ignoring found their voice, altering the course of my life in a surprising and wonderful way. For anyone contemplating having a go, let go of any preconceived ideas you may have, dive in and see what comes."

Frances Matthews,
Leadership & Development Consultant, www.qlearning.com

"This book combines wonderful story-telling with a precisely articulated emergent process to follow – alone or with others. If you're someone like me who enjoys plenty of underpinning theory and evidence to explain how and why the process of intuitive vision boarding works, at both the physiological and psychological level, you'll find this too. Mary Nondé's approach induces the right expansive state of mind that was a bit hit and miss for me when making a vision board on my own. I also found the advice on illumination and integration especially helpful since, without that application, it can remain simply a fun exercise.

"This book is a treasure and I anticipate everyone I know will be receiving a gift copy while my own will be much-loved and well-thumbed."

Kenda Gaynham,
Senior Facilitator, www.meetingmagic.com

"This book is powerful and revelatory. It highlighted to me the unacknowledged path I now wish to tread. For me this book speaks of passion, a deep passion for life, and for what life represents. I have not yet made a vision board, but I am now charged to do so having read this. My life has dramatically shifted this past year with my husband diagnosed with a critical condition. But this book inspires hope for me to entertain possibilities for myself and my family I never knew existed."

Karen Cunningham-Walker,
Facilities & Administrative Manager, PCS Instruments

"Reading *Awaken Your Intuitive Vision* brought my own board to life again as I now understand the depth and magic behind the process. While exploring Mary's unique personal and professional journey, I started to see things in a new light, recognising the signs and appreciating the mystery unfolding in my own life. I am so grateful for Mary's vision and how she guides us so gently to our own. This book has shared a truth, helping me believe that this process of self-development can support me in manifesting my life dreams. Beautifully written, warmly received, grateful I am to Mary for planting the seed."

Siri Arti,
Specialist Yoga Therapist, www.starchildyoga.com

"A heart-warming and amusing study of how Mary overcame severe adversity with a powerful, yet intensely spiritual mind and a unique process, always with the courage of her convictions. It is not 'rags to riches'; there are too many of those. With *Awaken Your Intuitive Vision* Mary offers a remarkable facility that not only enriches her own life, but has helped many others achieve something akin to their wildest dreams. In truth, I do not have the inherent control over my own left brain to contemplate preparing an Intuitive Vision Board without Mary's help. What is certain however, is that with my new-found awareness of Mary's methods, I will be attending an Intuitive Vision Board workshop in the very near future."

Michael Pattrick,
Entrepreneur

"If making the most of your one wild and wonderful life appeals to you, then you won't be disappointed by this book. Mary Nondé writes beautifully and the words flow and inspire. This book will teach you how to make sense of what you need to lead a happy life. This is an inspirational guide to tapping into your creative right brain to solve the challenges that life throws at you. Awakening your intuition to reach your potential – I couldn't put it down."

Kate Pichon,
Marketing Communications Consultant, Sunflower Consulting Services

"Mary takes us on a fascinating voyage into the unconscious in *Awaken Your Intuitive Vision.* The process is beautifully laid out in her book, with clear reasoning behind how it works and her lively, engaging style is inspiring and motivational – you'll be wanting to create your own vision before you get to the end. Mary's skill and wisdom takes you on a magical journey to meet your most magnificent self."

Sharon Whittock,
Image Consultant & Fashion Feng Shui™ Stylist, www.sharonwhittock.co.uk

"Mary Nondé writes with clarity and warmth. Her story-telling is lovely. From describing her own misfortunes to those of her case studies, she never fails to invoke sympathy for the situations, and joy for the successes the Intuitive Vision Board brings about. You cannot help but root for her and the clients whom she has worked with. It's a great read. Mary's explanations of how a vision board works are spot on having experienced making one myself. In fact, I valued being able to reference back to my own vision board with the explanations she had given. I thoroughly enjoyed reading this book."

Helen Foster,
www.helenfostercoaching.co.uk

"Mary's book is a truly creative and honest piece of writing as she shares her journey from surviving despair to connecting with her true nature and wisdom with the Intuitive Vision Board; it was like having coffee with a dear friend. I soaked up her beautiful stories and inspiring anecdotes as she took me on a journey of joyful creation, encouraging me to be open and receive the many possibilities for my 'one wild and wonderful life'. I enjoyed reading it even more the second time around."

Emily Wright,
www.findingstillness.co.uk

"In the best tradition of survival stories, Mary's journey gives rise to a practical philosophy for self-direction and navigation encapsulated in her wonderful book. Her unique approach to vision boarding has created a long overdue cultural shift in guided self-discovery. *Awaken Your Intuitive Vision* is the only book that will tell you how to read and interpret a vision board and how you too can become a 'heart-led visionary' for self-actualisation. You need this."

Lamia Walker,
CEO, www.housesitmatch.com

"The book carries a brilliant message for seekers, both conservative and liberal, sceptics and spiritual, basically anyone who is contemplating that something else."

Anna Pilon,
Spiritual seeker

"*Awaken Your Intuitive Vision* is beautifully written in a warm, engaging and intimate style. The reader is taken on a journey to explore how the unconscious mind works and how it encourages you to live the life you want to live. There are many parts in Mary's book I could totally relate to. I learned about the hardships Mary went through to get to the point in her life where she completely turned her life around for the better using the Intuitive Vision Board. You also read some amazing narratives from Mary's clients about their own positive life transformations, by attending the Intuitive Vision Board workshop.

For me personally, it was one of the very best things I could ever have done while the book shows you how to create your own Intuitive Vision Board. Pretty much 90% of my board has come true without even trying. It only goes to show that everything is possible."

Anabel Rowe,
Homemaker Extraordinaire

"Mary Nondé writes with hope, honesty and humour. In her inspirational and informative book, *Awaken Your Intuitive Vision*, Mary reveals the power of Intuitive Vision Boards and the intuition. She shares how this particular combination can empower us in times of uncertainty and change. Mary's creative process of working with Intuitive Vision Boards is well worth the exploration. I highly recommend this book and attending one of Mary's Intuitive Vision Board workshops too."

Mary Fraser,
Personal Development Coach

"I knew within the first few sentences of Mary Nondé's book that it would be one that would capture both my heart and mind, with tears in my eyes as her story unfolded of how she came to be the creator of the Intuitive Vision Board. Touching on her own experience and that of others using the Intuitive Vision Board, she shows how it can guide you through what can sometimes seem like a dark place called life.

"Mary explains in great detail how to create your own Intuitive Vision Board from the optimal space within. She explains the reasons why the Intuitive Vision Board produces deeper meaning and insights over other vision boards created from a list of wants. Engaging, inspiring, heartfelt and a 'must read' for those wishing to tap into their intuition to manifest their true desires in the outer world."

Lisa Walker,
www.lifeslittlepuzzles.com